CU01426258

Running the World

Running the World

A Runner's Odessey of Struggle and Triumph in the World Marathon Majors

Robyn Godfrey

All rights reserved.

No part of this publication may be reproduced, distributed, or transmitted in any form or by any means, including photocopying, recording, or other electronic or mechanical methods, without the prior written permission of the publisher, except as permitted by U.S. copyright law. For permission requests, contact Robyn Godfrey

For privacy reasons, some names, locations, and dates may have been changed.

Book Cover Photo by Robyn Godfrey

1st edition 2025

ISBN 9798313092928

Ebook ISBN

When you want something, all the universe conspires in helping you to achieve it.

Paulo Coelho *The Alchemist*

Table of Contents

Chapter 1 – How It Started

My feet pounded out a steady tempo against the pavement, muscles stiff and lungs rebelling as I settled into the first half mile of my run. Barely past 5:00 a.m., the North Carolina morning air was already heavy with heat and humidity, the sky still pitch-black. I kept the pace, enjoying the early morning solitude as I ran down the middle of Wilmington's normally busy streets, now quiet and empty of traffic.

Since I started running in 2013, certain routes had become second nature. The distances between locations like Whole Foods and McDonald's, Starbucks and the beach, home, and the park were easy to calculate. That morning, I took one of those familiar paths, and after a few miles, I found a rhythm. Traffic was light as I crossed major intersections. A podcast blared through my phone speaker. I didn't use headphones in case someone tried to abduct me. Of course, I listened to a true crime episode, which put me on edge, but I'm addicted. For defense, I kept a trusty fork in my pocket, ready for muggers, slashers, or local serial killers lurking at this hour. Yes, a fork. A friend in law enforcement had recommended it as a weapon, and it also served as a food utensil in case I needed a snack.

Once my breathing steadied, I began to enjoy the run. I'd read that the first mile is a liar, but for me, it was always the first two miles. I was a slow starter, not only at running but in most things in life. Waking up at 4:00 a.m. to start running by 5:00 a.m. made me chuckle; I used to come home from partying at that hour. Now, I was training for my second marathon.

Never athletic or sporty, I grew up tall, lanky, and uncoordinated. My dad used to say I had "knobby knees," and my mom called me a "klutz." They were right. I acquired it through honest means.

Movement, however, called from an early age. I grew up in Kansas City and used to love riding my bike around the suburbs, pedaling hard up the hills and gliding down with ease. Back then, my bike was a constant companion. My sparkly purple ten-speed with bright white taped handlebars brought a sense of liberation and freedom to roam to the library, the A&P grocery store, or friends' houses. As kids, we spent our days outside, only coming in when our parents called us for lunch or dinner. No TVs or video games as distractions, we stayed outside until the streetlights flicked on.

While biking came naturally, coordinating arms and legs on land seemed beyond me. Any attempt at catching, kicking, or hitting a ball resulted in tripping over my own feet. When playing kickball, volleyball, softball, or tennis my eye-hand coordination was practically nonexistent. Team captains never called my name first, second, or third. In those moments, frustration and sadness weighed heavily. I longed to belong, to be part of a group, a team, but my lack of athletic skills kept me on the outside.

Back in the '70s, physical education classes required kids to run six hundred yards or little less than a half mile. You'd think we were being asked to traverse hundreds of miles in the desert without food or water. Everyone dreaded it because, let's be honest, none of us were runners, and six hundred yards felt like an eternity. We'd huff and puff, gasping for breath as if we were about to meet our maker on the track.

I always came in last, slowly shuffling along while the PE teacher, who seemed to take pleasure in our misery, wrote down our times. I hated every second of it. I didn't like being sweaty, and I definitely didn't like him scribbling my time on that clipboard. I would have preferred to engage in almost any other activity, even algebra!

Because I wanted to thrive as a social butterfly in a world where my athletic abilities felt like an unavoidable flaw, my report cards and parent-teacher conferences echoed the same critiques: "Talks too much" and "daydreams in class." I longed to socialize, to be part of a team, but my lack of athleticism felt like a neon sign flashing "not a natural."

Eighth-grade basketball tryouts were a disaster. Dribbling, running, and shooting demanded coordination I simply didn't have. Next, I decided to try volleyball, but lacking the ability to move my body in an agile way made making contact with the ball seem impossible.

Sure, a bit of coaching and practice might have helped, but we didn't have today's resources to turn kids into sports stars. The formula stated that you either had the ability or you didn't, and that's how coaches chose teams.

In those days, track offered the unique freedom of no "tryouts" required. You could choose to "go out" for track without fearing that they would cut you for not being fast enough. At track meets, being the slowest runner didn't come with judgment. There wasn't pressure to set the world on fire; no one counted on me for a dramatic, game-winning moment. It felt like the one sport where showing up and running at my own pace didn't make me any less part of the team. If I tripped over my own feet or ran like a tortoise on sedatives, it hardly made a dent in the outcome of the meet.

Our track team had amazing sprinters, hurdlers, and middle-distance runners. I felt like a backup dancer at a pop concert important, but not the star. Sprinting? Definitely not my forte. Hurdling? Let's say my coordination made it a recipe for calamity. So, I stuck to the longer distances: the six hundred, the eight hundred, and the mile.

Once I started running, the six-hundred-yard PE requirement felt effortless. No more walking, no more finishing last. The coach's clipboard hardly registered in my mind anymore. Sweat didn't bother me it actually felt good, and soon I realized I could run farther than six hundred yards. After track practice, I often ran more on my own. Running became my escape, a way to break free from the house and move my body. It felt liberating, and the best part was I could do it. I learned to control my breath, find a rhythm, and pace myself for longer distances.

Once high school started, my running stopped, and my bike gathered dust, but my social life took off. I joined the marching band, but, come to find out, marching band demanded a *lot* of coordination. Playing an instrument while marching in time with the band and hitting a mark on a football field wasn't for the clumsy or uncoordinated.

Mr. Phipps, the band director, stood on a deer stand placed in the middle of a football field. His eagle eyes never missed anything. One misstep, and he started yelling at students to basically get their heads out of their asses. He spent half his time rolling his eyes and yelling at me through his bullhorn for always going the wrong way. "Robyn! Do you know your left from your right?" I cringed when he yelled my name. "How many times do I have to tell you to go right at the hashmark?" he'd holler. Being singled out embarrassed me, but I also felt bad for Mr. Phipps. I was there to socialize, and he was there to win band competitions.

Despite my awkwardness, I felt bold enough to try out for cheerleading my senior year. I wasn't as good as the cheerleaders on Netflix or *Bring It On*, but I could jump, do splits, and turn a cartwheel.

The last year of high school rolled around, bringing with it the legendary senior ski trip. What seemed like an innocent, fun-filled adventure ended up being a complete disaster. As an adult, I eventually developed a passion for snow skiing after taking lessons and actually learning how to ski. But as a high school kid, I didn't understand the value of proceeding with caution. Instead, I sped forward with no experience, following my friends up a mountainside. It brought to life the old adage, "If Jane jumps off a cliff, does that mean you will too?" When it came to me as a teenager, the answer was yes.

About seventy high schoolers crammed onto two yellow buses and embarked on a wild winter journey across the Kansas plains to the Colorado Rockies. The ride felt long and grueling, plagued by wind and snow, and little sleep along the way. Ice encrusted the windows, and a cold draft swept through the aisle, making the bus ride even less comfortable.

The buses rattled along through the dead of night, the engine hum filling the silence. Occasionally, laughter broke through the sleep-deprived haze. We knew we were starting something big, a real adventure. Mixed with excitement and fatigue, everyone traded stories about the mountains we would soon conquer. Despite the discomforts, an undeniable sense of camaraderie filled the bus. We were all on this crazy trip together, bundled in layers, trying to rest as the bus made its way toward the mountains.

After what felt like an eternity, snow-covered peaks appeared on the horizon. We had reached the Rockies, bleary-eyed but eager to hit the slopes. Little did I know, the real lesson of the trip wouldn't come from skiing but from my choice to jump in headfirst without fully understanding what I was getting into.

The first night, altitude sickness and dehydration took over, and it felt like a snowplow had run over me. I crawled to the kitchen on hands and knees and chugged glass after glass of water, hoping my headache would fade.

The next day, we outfitted ourselves in boots, poles, and skis, ready or so I thought to take on the slopes. My friend Becky and I, both first-timers, decided to skip the bunny slope, as all beginners should (no, not really!), and instead, we followed the crowd. We made our way to a ski lift to an intermediate "blue" run.

"Shouldn't we take a lesson or something?" I asked as we made our way clumsily to the lift line, following our friends.

"It can't be that hard. We'll figure it out," she said.

We had no idea how to even get on a ski lift, let alone ski. I almost knocked everyone off the platform with my flailing arms and lack of control. Once on the lift, as we started to climb up the mountain, unease took over. The higher we went, the more I worried. We had no plan on how to get back to the base without dying or, worse, embarrassing ourselves. With each minute we climbed, my anxiety grew. I didn't know how we were going to dismount without crashing.

As the lift neared the top, my panic rose. When we reached the unloading area, my heart rate shot up to a hundred. I knew something had to happen, but fear gripped me. I tried to stand up and step off the lift, but as my skis hit the snow, I stumbled and took a nosedive. The chairlift smacked me in the back of the head (this was before helmets became standard). Then came my grand finale: a full-on "yard sale," that's ski lingo for when you fall off the lift, your skis, poles, and gear scattering in all directions. The lift operators usually stop the lift to help you collect your things and clear the area, but there I was, sprawled in the snow, the entire lift audience watching my spectacular failure. Laughter echoed around me. I could hear the snickers as everyone mocked my poor attempt at skiing. I felt like I was in a comedy skit. I couldn't help but laugh at myself, too, but I also wanted to crawl into a snowbank and never come out.

I give myself credit for my commitment and my willingness to try, but the reality of skiing became apparent. I started down the mountain, screaming my head off, out of control, and heading for a cliff. I didn't know how to stop, so I headed for a tree. Slam! The impact sent a sharp pain through my left knee. Unable to stand up, tears streamed down my face as the pain intensified. My friends called ski patrol, and Becky stayed with me, trying to keep me calm.

Once ski patrol arrived, they loaded me onto a stretcher and carried me off the mountain. As embarrassing as it felt, I was relieved I didn't have to ski down the rest of the slope. Becky shared that sentiment, too.

"These ski patrol guys are super cute," she said as we motored down the mountain. I chuckled and tried to enjoy the ride, my teenage-self appreciating being rescued by handsome ski patrol guys.

At the condos, I nursed my knee, now in a brace from hip to ankle. My body felt like it had been through a war zone, and I was still battling altitude sickness. I hung around the hot tub, listening to everyone swap stories about their day on the slopes. I loved the tales and wished I could've skied like the others. I mentally chided myself for not going to the bunny slope. Meanwhile, we stayed warm and tried to forget the chaos of my first day of skiing.

It wasn't the glorious adventure I envisioned, but it began my journey with skiing. It also taught me to think about my limits. I was never so glad to get back to Kansas City and a "normal" altitude.

Once home, this escapade led to a trip to an orthopedic doctor. Arthroscopic knee surgery was new at that time, and my doctor urged me to go ahead with it, promising little to no aftereffects. After surgery, I spent a few weeks on crutches and then was "free to resume" activities. My knee was never the same again.

Even with my crazy antics in marching band, poor cheerleading skills, and a harrowing ski trip, I survived high school. After graduating in May of 1984, I began attending Central Missouri State University (now the University of Central Missouri). College turned out to be a game changer. Once away at school, the taste of freedom hit me like a drug. I had all the distractions a college kid could dream of: I joined a sorority, began drinking beer, and took up smoking. My diet became a glorious tribute to junk food. I consumed pizza, fries, fast food, Diet Coke, and potato chips like a champion.

I can't claim to have made the best choices as a college student. I'm not the first nor last person to experience this. I was still thin, lanky, and klutzy but in no way healthy. I smoked a pack a day, drank way too much beer, and never touched a vegetable or fruit unless it was in my drink. My only form of exercise during my college career was walking to class and dancing the night away.

After college, ready to tackle the world, I packed my bags and moved to the Washington, DC metro area. I dropped my cigarette habit, joined the local Bally's Fitness Center, and quickly developed a passion for aerobics. Aerobics was the hottest ticket in town during the late '80s and early '90s. Leotard-clad women, who looked like they were auditioning for a Jane Fonda video, packed the group exercise classes. All were eager to crank up their endorphins and burn calories. My girlfriend and I would show up three days a week for an instructor who seemed to have a PhD in yelling. We were sure she hated everyone in the room, but her classes turned us into sweaty puddles of determination. I discovered with astonishment that aerobics was the antidote to my clumsiness. Doing the steps, jumps, and side-to-side moves while waving my arms built some rhythm and coordination.

As the years rolled by, I met my husband Scott, got married, and moved to North Carolina, where I dove headfirst into a career in sales. Though I traveled a lot for work, my metabolism was like a well-oiled machine and kept me slim. Sure, I picked up an extra ten pounds at thirty and another five at thirty-five, but I was tall enough to play hide-and-seek with the weight.

I tried counting calories, but that lasted about as long as a New Year's resolution. I still enjoyed my beer but added wine and the occasional cocktail to the mix, completely overlooking those calories. Being in sales meant entertaining customers, going out for dinners, drinking wine, indulging in desserts, and having late nights followed by early mornings. It felt like living in a never-ending party, and I loved every second of it.

The job was stressful and after a nightmare of a trip, I would often drown my frustrations in wine and food, hoping for a cure-all. I would still hit the gym after these nights of indulging, but I soon realized I couldn't out-exercise my eating and drinking habits.

I woke up one day and realized, at forty years of age, I felt pudgy for the first time in my life. I joked with my sister-in-law that I "weighed more than I ever had." Sure, I wanted to lose weight and be slimmer. But change my bad habits? No, thank you. I would try to eat healthy for a few days, but then a coworker or friend would suggest happy hour, dinner, or partying after work, and I would abandon my plan and devour fried food, chips, salsa, tacos, and margaritas. My decision-making skills were on vacation. Deep down, I wanted my metabolism back, but I didn't want to change my habits or worse, diet.

One morning, on a business trip in Tampa, I woke up feeling terrible after a late night out with clients and colleagues. Bloated, heavy, foggy nothing about me felt right. I looked in the mirror and wondered if I had a problem with alcohol. Shame washed over me for not being able to avoid social situations where I overindulged. The person staring back at me looked like hell, and that made me sad, depressed, and miserable.

After a night of partying in my twenties and thirties, all I had to do was guzzle a bottle of water, hang my head off the bed, and wash my face in cold water to make the dark circles and puffy eyes disappear and youthful skin spring back. Those techniques, while creative, were not working anymore. My bad habits were catching up to me and showing on my face and my thighs.

During that Tampa trip, after only three hours of sleep and suffering from a hangover that felt like a marching band in my head, I decided to put on workout clothes and go to the hotel gym. My goal? Get on the treadmill and wake up. In my bedhead glory, for reasons I can't quite explain, I thought, *Let's try running for thirty seconds*. Even though I hadn't run a step since my early high school track days, that morning, I jogged on the treadmill. Within seconds, sweat poured out of me, and I could hardly breathe, but it felt detoxifying, as my body flushed out the rich food and cocktails.

Once the thirty seconds of pure panic were over, I switched to walking and gave myself a little pep talk. Five minutes later, I started running for another thirty seconds. I did this for a half hour, alternating between dripping sweat and fearing I would vomit. By the end, I felt much better, more alert, and had more energy. Would this be the beginning of my running journey and ultimate transformation? I wish I could say I dramatically changed my lifestyle. I didn't start eating kale for breakfast, cut back on alcohol, or get more sleep. I had a bad case of FOMO (fear of missing out) and felt I needed to be at every event, dinner, party, and gathering with people, food, and drinks.

Still, that treadmill experience did light a fire under me. I started running and walking at my local Gold's Gym. I would kick off with thirty seconds of running followed by two minutes of walking on the treadmill. My version of a jog and a leisurely stroll. I increased the running duration to forty-five seconds, and before I realized it, I was running for a full minute, followed by a minute of walking. Progress!

I worked my way up to four miles using this interval method, which started my endurance training and breath control. I didn't know that alternating between pretending to run and strolling could boost my fitness. During this time, I played tennis, followed by tacos after matches. Old habits die hard. Even so, the extra calorie burn started to have an effect. I began to slim down and felt my muscles get firmer and more toned. The endorphins gave me a great post-workout high.

Out of the blue, my friend Sheila popped the question: "Do you want to run the Cooper River 10K Bridge Run in Charleston, South Carolina for fun?"

Me? Run? A real race? I mean, a girls' weekend in Charleston, that's a definite "yes, duh"! Though 6.2 miles felt like an eternity, I jumped at the chance without a second thought. Of course, I had no idea what I'd gotten myself into (cue flashbacks to the ski trip disaster). At that time, I had run outside only for school track. My primary experience with running was indoors on the treadmill for a couple of miles. I didn't consider myself a "real runner." *How on earth would I run six miles?*

Chapter 2 – Becoming a "Real Runner"

I've always had what I call "Type A Personality Syndrome" ambitious, organized, high-achieving, spontaneous, stubborn, and a bit crazy. This mix of traits drives me but also creates challenges. I thrive on structure, ceaselessly chasing goals, but rarely show myself any compassion. Deciding to run a 10K only amplified these tendencies.

Was I apprehensive about running 6.2 miles? Maybe. But doing it halfway? Not an option. If I was going to run a 10K, it had to be like a "real runner." Somewhere, I had picked up the odd belief that to be a legitimate "real runner," I had to be faster than everyone and collect medals. Later, as I grew into my running practice, this belief would be reevaluated, but, at that moment, my Type A personality saw this opportunity as a motivating challenge. I could and would do this. Without hesitation, I signed up. I signed up so early, in fact, that the race organizers assigned me to Corral A, the starting area directly behind the elite athletes. Elite athletes are runners who are so much faster than everyone else. They start, finish, shower, and eat breakfast while the rest of us are at mile three. At the time, there was no way of knowing I would be in front of forty thousand people running one of the biggest 10Ks in the country and forever transformed.

My training began with running outside. Running outdoors proved to be a completely different experience than the treadmill. There's wind, temperature, traffic, uneven terrain, different surfaces, and inclines, but also beauty and fresh air. It was tough at first; all these factors slowed me down and made the effort seem more difficult. (Spoiler: the effort *felt* harder.) I was no longer running in a controlled environment. No A/C, no fan, no treadmill to maintain my pace, and no "stop" button to make the discomfort vanish.

I downloaded a run app to my phone that would tell me my pace and how far I had gone from my starting point. On my first day outside, starting from my front door, I ran for a half mile, turned around, and came back. I did this for several weeks, eventually working my way up to 1.5 miles out and back. I lived near the University of North Carolina Wilmington (UNCW), which gave me access to campus paths. I calculated how far key points on the campus were from my house and started to think about going farther and farther just to see how long I could go. Could I run all the way around campus from my front door and make it back? It was about a 4.5-mile loop and seemed formidable.

I still played a lot of tennis, as it served as my social outlet, but I began to notice that all the running actually made me faster on the court. However, the unintended side effect made me lose interest in tennis. Tennis demanded so much mental effort, and my mind often wandered to more pressing matters, like what I'd have for dinner. As for my hand-eye coordination? Let's just say it didn't magically improve despite hours of practice and years of taking lessons from various tennis pros, attending clinics, and daily play. Scott joked that I'd invested all this time and money into my tennis game and still hadn't made the cut for Wimbledon.

Tennis became increasingly competitive, with players sometimes resorting to catty behavior or even cheating to win. The constant pressure to decide which team I'd be on, the expectation to win, and the guilt of losing wore me out. Ultimately, I just wanted to chat and be social. I shifted away from tennis and turned to running. Despite the seeming contradiction, running was easier on my body. It freed me from the aches and pains of tennis elbow, sore knees from the side-to-side court movement, and swollen ankles from rolling them on the hard court.

My tennis friend, Diane, also ran and invited me to join her local running club. The first night, I felt totally out of my league. It was the day after the 2013 Boston Marathon bombing, the tragic attack that killed three people and injured hundreds. We all gathered, joined hands, and observed a moment of silence for the victims. I felt like a fraud. Who was I to take part in this solemn moment when I didn't truly consider myself a runner?

These were the "real runners" the kind who looked like they belonged on the cover of *Runner's World*. Lean, fit, clad in sports bras and running shorts, moving with the easy confidence of people who knew their pace down to the second. They wore fancy watches and spoke in a language of races, paces, and finishing times. Meanwhile, I stood there in a pair of secondhand Brooks from Goodwill, cotton socks, and a mismatched tank and shorts from the clearance rack at TJ Maxx. When I first saw the price of running shoes, I balked seventy-five dollars for sneakers? Forty dollars for shorts? Absolutely not. At the time, I had no idea what a little thing like fabric choice could mean for a runner. I had yet to make the painful acquaintance of chafing.

While standing there, taking it all in and trying to figure out how I would survive this outing, Nicole, the prettiest, leanest, and most fit female in the group, started talking about her recent half marathon. She was funny and engaging, and I couldn't help but be drawn in by her. She recounted how she sat down mid-race and had a full-blown temper tantrum, complete with crying and fit-throwing.

"I was running, and all of a sudden, I started crying, and I sat down on the curb and bawled my eyes out for no reason," she explained. "I was so mad!" She half chuckled, and everyone else laughed, too. I didn't know running could be so dramatic.

She went on to explain that she didn't know why she did this, and while she laughed at herself, I could tell it bothered her. Her story touched me, and I wondered why running would cause her to have these reactions. I didn't yet know that heart rate and other factors can wreak havoc on emotions. Since that day, Nicole has not only become my friend, but she has also conquered her emotions and runs marathons and ultras like a boss.

They say you never know who you're inspiring, and it's true. Nicole made me realize it's okay to not be perfect. I looked at her, fit and "like a runner," and assumed she had everything figured out. That night, I ran with the group, and while I might've been the last to finish, it didn't matter I was running. I felt incredible afterward, chatting and making new friends. Right there, I joined the Wilmington Road Runners Club. It helped that it was pizza night (because carbs, right?). That experience taught me to encourage other runners to join a club. Turns out, your best friends are waiting there. And I found mine.

After a year of training (yes, you read that right) and shedding a few pounds, I stood among forty thousand runners in Mount Pleasant, South Carolina, behind the elite athletes. When the gun went off, we surged forward, heading toward the on-ramp of the Ravenel Bridge that spans the Cooper River into Charleston. The incline on the Mount Pleasant side hits a steep 5.6 percent grade difficult, but I refused to walk. Once we crested the bridge, the downhill rush felt incredible, with the wind whipping past. I continued through the streets of downtown Charleston, surrounded by cheering crowds that made me feel like this was the Olympics. I couldn't wipe the smile off my face. Bands blared upbeat tunes along the course, and spectators held signs like "Don't trust a fart" solid advice, indeed!

As we neared the finish line, the massive crowds cheered for us like we were about to win gold. Crossing that line, I felt like I was walking on air. At forty-six, I had just completed my first 10K in 55:56; I became an official runner with a finisher's medal to prove it. I couldn't wait to tell everyone even my dentist got the news. "Oh, by the way, I ran a 10K last week, that's 6.2 miles." Little did I know, Cooper River would hold my 10K personal best for years to come.

Once I crossed that finish line, I craved more. Not just running but getting better at it. I started racing in local 5Ks with my run club, landing in second or third place in my age group. I learned what a "Masters Runner" was (over forty) and what it took to be a "Grand Master" (over fifty). With each race, I pushed my limits, often hating the discomfort but somehow loving the challenge.

Running was easy in theory but hard in practice. My lungs burned, and my mind screamed to stop, but I kept going. It became addictive, and even though I couldn't wait for the finish line, I yearned for the next race. One of my favorites became the Tri Span 10K in downtown Wilmington, a brutal race in July, crossing three main bridges. The heat, the inclines, the mental grind it was all tough, but I loved every minute of it.

After conferring with my new running family, we set our sights on conquering a half marathon, a distance of 13.1 miles.

By then, I'd been running officially since April 2013, and I was ready to push myself to the next level. Fall 2014 would be the perfect time to run my first half.

Wilmington offers several top-notch half marathons, but one stands out: the Battleship Half Marathon, a local tradition for about twenty-five years. Sitting moored along the Cape Fear River is the USS *North Carolina*, a battleship commissioned in 1941 and a key player in World War II. Decommissioned and transferred to North Carolina in 1961, the battleship, now a memorial and museum, sits proudly across from our historic waterfront impossible to miss unless you're too busy looking at your phone.

Tackling the Battleship Half Marathon in November 2014 meant training through a North Carolina summer for the first time. Southeastern North Carolina's heat and humidity were unforgiving, leaving us drenched in sweat after just a few miles. Our running routes, unfamiliar and full of twists, often had us feeling lost like a group of tourists wandering through an unknown city. We were clueless about fueling, which led to some serious gastrointestinal distress. *Bridesmaids* movie-moments were almost a reality. I vividly remember sitting down on the road, convinced I wouldn't make it to the bathroom in time and repeating, "Please don't let this be happening!" Nothing says "serious runner" quite like a public bathroom emergency.

Training became an adventure of its own. We got lost, hit the wall, sweated through every pore, and endured constant GI distress. Each run felt like a comedy of errors. But through the sweat, laughter, and occasional panic, we stayed determined to make it to race day. We blissfully ignored most of the details like nutrition, hydration, and figuring out running routes.

I bought the cheapest Garmin watch I could find, only to discover I needed to "wait for satellites" before running to be sure every step was recorded. I turned it on and off every time I stopped at lights, watching the time slip away in frustration. But despite all the training hiccups, it felt glorious. My legs grew stronger and lighter. I shed pounds, and my body became leaner and fitter than I ever imagined.

I'll never forget running ten miles for the first time. The pride I felt was electric. I was buzzing from that exhilarating runner's high and practically floated home. In celebration, I devoured an entire pizza, leaving Scott in shock and awe. My days on the tennis court faded into the background as I discovered a new tribe in the running community. Running became my escape, a chance to explore new places whether on a business trip or right outside my front door. It felt like being a kid again, discovering the world with every stride.

We did our long runs every Sunday from Whole Foods. We laughed and built friendships along the way. We ran through heat, thunderstorms, before dawn or through the blazing sun, and no topic was off-limits. We talked about our jobs, families, politics, food, running, and yes bodily functions. There was even the time we ran in a tropical storm and ended up being interviewed by The Weather Channel for our audacity! Nothing felt impossible. With each run, whether on trails, roads, bike paths, or sandy shores, I built resilience, mental toughness, and fitness one step at a time.

The day before the Battleship Half Marathon, we picked up our race packets and our race bibs. Mine said, "First Half Marathon." We snapped photos of each other, laughed, and joked about our summer training sessions. The night before the race, we gathered for pasta at a local Italian restaurant and talked about running. We were pumped to crush it the next day.

At that time, the race started at Battleship Park, which offered a striking view of the USS North Carolina. From there, runners headed north, crossing the Rhodes Bridge, which gracefully spans wetlands and tributaries a prime spot to catch a glimpse of the occasional alligator. The course then took us over the Isabel Holmes Bridge on the north side of downtown, crossing the Cape Fear River. While not quite the Rocky Mountains, the course featured gradual inclines and declines that gave your legs a mini workout with every step.

Since these bridges have no pedestrian walkways and are major traffic routes, practice runs were not an option. On race day, organizers closed off one lane of traffic, giving us the space we needed to run safely without dodging cars while gasping for air. The course wound through downtown Wilmington and Greenfield Lake Park before culminating in crossing the Cape Fear Memorial Bridge on the south side of town. This bridge, with its intimidating metal grates, had claimed more than a few shins, hands, and faces from runners who tripped along the way. As we approached it, we couldn't help but question our life choices as we focused on keeping our footing.

The weather on race day had turned windy and bitter cold. Unfazed, I pinned my bib excitedly. I carpooled with my friend Amanda and connected with my training group for a quick picture while we tried to stay warm. We lined up at the start, shed our "throwaway" clothes, and sang the national anthem, all while shivering violently. I plugged in my earbuds for some background music, then the gun went off, and we launched into running. The group started out together, calling to each other as we ran. As the race went on, we began to drift apart, some running faster, some slower than others. We let each other go but wished each other well. Our run club set up aid stations and cheered us on. I felt the support of the new friends I had made. At around mile five, I started warming up and made the rookie mistake of throwing away my gloves. We were two bridges down and entering Greenfield Park, a four-mile running path around a lake. It's a beautiful part of Wilmington that many runners and cyclists use year-round. I grabbed water and fuel at the aid stations and kept on running.

At mile ten, as I ran out of the park fighting against the blustery wind, my hands now frozen, fatigue set in. Once we climbed the on-ramp to the Cape Fear Memorial Bridge, the wind howled, and I felt like I was standing still. I couldn't wait to finish so I could escape the cold. We crested the top of the bridge, and I started to "smell the barn," pushing the pace. I hauled ass to the finish line and ran my heart out, finishing in 2:02. Exhilarated, but the coldest I had ever been in my life, I couldn't believe I did it. I ran a half marathon! Active military personnel handed out the finisher medals at the end of the race, honoring us all for our feats. Elated and proud to get my first half marathon medal, I finally felt like a "real runner."

I fell in love with the half marathon distance and, like a lunatic, signed up for four more the following year. As I racked up races, I started snagging age-group awards and uncovering just how much running could offer friends, adventures, and endless discoveries. Running turned my work trips into mini adventures. On chilly mornings, I'd bundle up and hit the streets of DC, weave through downtown Chicago, or dash from a Hilton Garden Inn in Colorado Springs. There's something magical about exploring on foot it allows you to notice the little things you'd miss zooming by in a car.

Members of the running club, non-running friends, coworkers, and family kept asking when I'd run a marathon. It felt like such a distant goal; 26.2 miles seemed overwhelming too long, too hard, and well beyond my reach. I couldn't imagine running for three, four, or five hours. I wasn't sure I could or even wanted to do it. It felt like a bridge too far.

Until, one day, it wasn't.

That's how I found myself out on the deserted streets of Wilmington in the pre-dawn hours, my footsteps echoing against the pavement, listening to true crime podcasts, and working toward a twenty-mile training run.

Somehow, I had gone from someone who looked in the mirror with shame for not being able to "just say no" to alcohol and lavish meals to a marathoner in the making.

Chapter 3 – London Calling

S ales in corporate America operated like a high-stakes pursuit, driven by relentless goals and fierce competition. Every month brought a new quota to hit, and the pressure mounted over the course of a year. It often felt like a battle on the African savannah, with teams locked in an ongoing scramble for a piece of meat, racing to outpace each other. Tensions ran high. The stakes never let up. Every victory required strategy and determination.

The key to meeting or exceeding a quota lies in breaking it down into manageable steps, having a clear plan, and executing the plan. For me, organization and execution became the driving forces behind success. I spent most of my career in sales in technical fields so complex that my parents and husband often found themselves scratching their heads when friends asked, "What does she do?" The usual answer was, "Something with computers?"

I discovered that marathoning had a surprising amount in common with being a salesperson, trying to meet quota in the corporate world. Both felt like monumental tasks at first and overwhelming in their scale. But once broken down into manageable steps, they resembled the age-old advice of how to eat an elephant, one bite at a time. Whether it was pacing myself through a long race or chipping away at a massive sales target, the recipe was the same: create a plan, focus on the next step, and execute the plan through the end.

Running gave me the chance to set goals and milestones *for me* not for a corporation or a boss, but for my own growth. Like in business, sometimes I'd miss my targets by a hair; other times, I'd win by a narrow margin. But every now and then, I'd crush them. That kept me coming back for more. For someone with "Type A" syndrome, it felt like a drug. Hitting and surpassing goals became addictive and transformative. I carried myself like a winner. I couldn't imagine living without that rush.

People asked me all the time when I planned to run a marathon. For me, it felt like a faraway dream. I enjoyed running various distances, but I also thrived on the training process. The discipline, the structure, and the tangible results all clicked with my personality. I loved setting goals, and training for a race became the perfect way to work toward and achieve something meaningful.

After the Battleship, I signed up for four half marathons in 2015. I trained all the time. I ran the beach on Mondays, hills on Tuesdays, track on Thursdays, from the coffee shop on Fridays, and from Whole Foods on Sundays. I ran with a subgroup of women in the run club that kept me going. We talked about our jobs, kids, husbands, family, home life, big and small decisions, careers, the meaning of life, GI distress, eating, drinking, and our pets. Nothing was off limits. We dressed up for our runs: zombies for Halloween runs, tutus for the Run for the Ta Tas, and ugly sweaters for Christmas runs. We had pancake runs, watermelon runs, beer runs, you name it, we ran for it or because of it. I even bought a hanger for all my race medals that were starting to stack up.

I can't remember the exact location, day, or time, but I do remember the conversation that led me to enter my first marathon. Naturally, we were out for a run and started talking about races that would be fun. We dreamed about running in the vineyards in California, the beautiful scenery of the Grand Tetons, and other locales. Then someone said, "Wouldn't it be amazing to run through the five boroughs of New York?" One person suggested, "Wouldn't it be incredible to run in Paris or Dublin or London?" *London.* London stuck with me. I was turning fifty the next year, and my mind started churning. I started asking myself, *Wouldn't it be a chance of a lifetime to run a marathon in London? Wouldn't it be an incredible accomplishment to run the London Marathon? Wouldn't it be epic to run the London Marathon for my fiftieth birthday?*

I've been obsessed with all things British my entire life. I devoured countless historical novels set in Regency England, starting in my early teens. I cherished the classics like *Jane Eyre, Pride and Prejudice, Emma,* and *Wuthering Heights*. In college, I dove into British Literature, British History, Scottish History, Irish History, Russian History anything related to European history. I didn't just read the trashy stuff; I immersed myself in every book I could find, whether it was classic literature or Regency romances with dashing men on the cover. I adored every movie, crime procedural, PBS mystery, or Acorn drama *Downton Abbey, The Crown, Broadchurch* you name it. History was my passion, and visiting London was the ultimate dream come true.

The birth of the modern-day marathon distance had been decided in the UK. The story goes that in 1908, during the Olympic Games in London, Queen Alexandria requested that the race start on the lawn of Windsor Castle and finish at the Royal Box of the Olympic stadium. Turns out that is exactly 26.2 miles. To this day, that is the official distance of the marathon. In the early days of marathoning, the distance fluctuated from race to race. The official marathon distance would not be confirmed until 1924 at the Paris Olympics.

That rich history loomed in the back of my mind as I began my own journey. Research ensued. *How do I run the London Marathon?* At the time, I had no idea just how competitive it would be. London, as I would soon learn, is one of the toughest marathons to enter. The odds felt almost impossible. With fifty thousand runners and two hundred thousand people entering the lottery, the race had also become one of the largest charity events in the world, raising millions of dollars each year. People from all over the globe dreamed of running it, and many had tried for years some for decades entering the lottery over and over, only to face rejection.

More Googling ensued, and I found Marathon Tours, a travel agency specifically for people who want to run marathons all over the world. Who knew there was such a thing? I certainly didn't. Lucky for me, they were advertising a lottery for a hundred runners to obtain entries into the London Marathon. I had to travel (and pay) with their group, but if selected, I would be guaranteed an entry. I thought about it over the next few days and finally just threw my name in. As was my previous M.O., I would figure things out later if I got accepted.

While my uncertainty lingered at having entered the lottery on a whim, by July 2015, it didn't matter anymore. I received an email telling me I was in. I was going to run my first-ever marathon. And in London, no less! I felt a mix of excitement and panic. I had no clue how to tackle a marathon, but the pull of running in London was enough to push me to figure it out. Fortunately, my running club had a whole team of experts who were ready to guide me.

Training for a marathon was all new to me. Like most first-time marathoners, I took to the web to find a training plan. *Runner's World* offered a plethora of plans for beginner marathoners. I closed my eyes and picked one. For the next sixteen weeks, I would be "in training." While I still enjoyed drinking wine and beer, I started to cut way back. I ate more vegetables and became more diligent about stretching, foam rolling, and sleeping. December 1, 2015, was a Tuesday and day one of training.

I quickly learned that winter training could be wonderful. I loved the cold mornings, bundling up to run, and hitting new distance milestones each week. The first time I ran fourteen miles at one time, I snapped a photo for Facebook to commemorate the occasion. I felt delirious after that run. I had no idea how I would manage to run more miles the following week, but seven days later, I found myself out there, completing sixteen miles, then eighteen miles the week after. I discovered that eighteen miles presented a real challenge for me. I struggled to finish and felt utterly depleted. After my long runs, I'd go home, eat, and collapse on the couch for the rest of the day. These distances had always seemed unreachable, though somehow I kept meeting targets week after week. I felt completely surprised by my progress but proud that I could actually complete the task.

I ran tempo runs, which were comfortably hard, faster than easy pace but not full sprints, track workouts, easy runs, and long runs every week. I ran while traveling for work, even when hungover and didn't want to, and I experienced fantastic runner's highs. My longest training run stretched to twenty-three miles during the annual River to Sea run in Wilmington. Wilmington lies along the Cape Fear River, but the town stretches all the way to Wrightsville Beach on the Atlantic Ocean about ten to eleven miles, depending on whose yard you run through and which fences you jump over.

With a twenty-mile run on my training plan, I decided to run "sea to river, river to sea." Accidentally, my group ran twenty-three miles with a few wrong turns and mixing in a bit of delirium. Exhausted but laughing, we stretched, took photos, and marveled at how far we'd run, all agreeing we must be crazy. Afterward, we headed to breakfast, and I devoured food like a starving animal. I turned down social activities, knowing I had to run again the next day.

"Sorry, I can't go out tonight. I've got to run tomorrow," became a repetitive statement. Who had I become? I barely recognized myself. Scott, along with many family members and friends, stood stunned. I seemed to be transforming before their eyes.

Remarkably, I met Pam, another runner in Wilmington training for London, and we began running together. She had several marathons under her belt and quickly became a "marathon mentor" to me. If I didn't have a great run, she made me feel better and reminded me to carb-load, stretch, and accept that feeling tired all the time came with the territory. Together, we pored over the course details and race logistics. During one of our training runs, she casually mentioned the "World Marathon Majors" and the "Six Star Medal." She was working her way through the races, with London as her next "star." I had never heard of the Six Star Medal and knew nothing about the World Marathon Majors. The more she talked about it, the more intrigued I became. Running in the world's greatest cities, experiencing them on foot through a marathon, and exploring places like Berlin, Tokyo, Boston, New York, and Chicago sounded like the goal of a lifetime. The seed was planted in my mind, but it would be a while before it sprouted. I needed to focus on training for the massive goal of finishing the London Marathon. Coincidentally, a business trip took me to London, Bath, and Portsmouth in mid-February 2016. I felt so excited despite traveling during the UK's worst weather month and amid massive flooding across Southern England. I didn't care; I was going to the UK, a dream come true even if it was a business trip.

Mesmerized, I gazed out the airplane window as we descended toward Heathrow Airport, my eyes drinking in the endless patchwork of green fields and neatly lined rows of trees beneath a gray, overcast sky. The landscape felt like a living postcard, so different from anything I had ever seen. Once we touched down, it didn't matter that the skies were dreary or that the rain and dampness clung to everything. I had finally set foot in England.

February in England clung to dark and gloomy like a season it would not outgrow. The sun doesn't rise until 8:00 a.m., and it sets by 4:00 p.m. The country's roads lacked bike paths, sidewalks, and shoulders; running on them felt dangerous, literally life-threatening. Still, I wanted to run. I tried using the hotel treadmill, but the conversion from kilometers to miles didn't compute in my head. On my second morning staying in Bath, I considered my life choices and chose to hit the streets. Sleet, freezing rain, cold, misery, and darkness awaited me. Yet, I ran. I passed the massive Bath Abbey, built in 1611, which dominated the city. I made my way through neighborhoods and city streets until I got so lost that I feared I'd never find my way back. My GPS failed to work because of the freezing rain, and I couldn't enter my passcode since my fingers had gotten so wet (this was before face recognition).

I quickly realized that all the buildings in Bath looked the same: white limestone with long, sweeping curves. My only saving grace came as I ran closer to the city center, where the pavers on the streets grew smaller and abbey spires stood visible for miles, beckoning me back to my starting point. I'll never forget that run. It prepared me for the weather in England and boosted my confidence. Freezing but smiling, I returned to my hotel eight miles later. My coworkers thought I'd lost my mind, but I had grown used to that by then. The next time I set foot in the UK, I'd be running the London Marathon.

Pam had bought me a book on the history of the London Marathon which I scoured. The London Marathon raises more money for charity than any other marathon and holds the Guinness World Record for biggest one-day fundraising event. On the lighter side of things, the race holds many Guinness World Records for wearing "fancy dress" while running a marathon. Fancy dress includes wearing attire like ball gowns, phone booths, or dinosaur costumes. The London Marathon race prides itself on not only being impactful to the world but also fun.

The 2016 London Marathon marked its thirty sixth running and became the year the millionth runner crossed the finish line. A massive campaign, "One in a Million," accompanied the event. The runner who crossed the line as the millionth finisher would gain notoriety, be featured in race marketing, and receive extra prizes. For social media, we raised one finger during training and at the finish line in photos, using the hashtag #oneinamillion to show we were all "one in a million."

The last two weeks before the race put me in "taper" mode, meaning I cut back on my mileage and rested my legs. Experienced runners warned me that I'd go crazy during tapering and lose my mind. According to Scott and my family, that had already happened. I found that I actually enjoyed the lessening of the needed mileage and savored the rest.

I completed my final speed workout with Nicole at the track, and in that moment, everything felt like it had come full circle. No longer the runner who felt like a fraud in used shoes and cotton clothes, I stood on the brink of one of the most prestigious marathons in the world, preparing to race through one of the most iconic cities on Earth. I no longer just ran. I had become an athlete something once beyond my reach, a dream I never imagined possible.

Chapter 4 – London Marathon 2016

I stepped out of the taxi at Wilmington Airport, surprised to see my running friends gathered with signs wishing me luck. They had taken time out of their day to come to the airport to see me off. Their thoughtfulness touched me deeply, and I realized that somewhere along the way, not only had I truly become a runner, but I also found a tribe. They helped build my resilience, pushing me to keep going when I doubted myself.

After tearful goodbyes and hugs, Scott and I grabbed our luggage and checked in. He joked about having to fly in coach for eight hours even though he wasn't the one running a marathon. Little did he know I had secured first-class seats for the trip. We boarded our connecting flight in Philadelphia, and as he started to head toward coach, I told him to turn left instead of right. His face lit up as a grin spread across it. Who knew a man could be so happy in a pod?

We were able to fully lie down and sleep while flying "across the pond". I ate dinner drank lots of water, watched *Chariots of Fire* for motivation and went to sleep. Scott decided to partake in all the amenities in first class on a trans-Atlantic flight. He had drinks, snacks, and ice cream at midnight, watched a half dozen action movies and didn't sleep a wink. He would later regret those decisions.

We touched down at Heathrow, dropped our bags at the hotel, hopped on the tube, and headed to the expo to pick up my race packet. The expo took place at the London Excel Convention Center in East London, past Greenwich. I remember taking a few trains to get there, feeling both exhausted and jetlagged but excited, too. The energy in all of London seemed to match my own. I picked up my bib, snapped a few photos, and cruised through the surprisingly small expo. Most race expos feature seasoned marathoners speaking on topics like nutrition and race strategy, along with heaps of merchandise, from gels and electrolytes to socks, sunglasses, branded T-shirts, jackets, tights, hats, and just about anything else you could imagine.

Booking with Marathon Tours (MT) turned out to be a genius move. Our hotel, located near the finish line in the heart of London, sat within walking distance of Big Ben, Buckingham Palace, Tower Bridge, and the London Eye. MT organized a guided tour of the city the next day, complete with a boat ride on the Thames and a visit to the Tower of London. Most of the tour took place on a bus, with the guide highlighting all the key sites, thus saving our legs. On the Thames, we gawked at Tower Bridge, knowing we would run across it at the halfway point of the marathon. The weather stayed brisk but beautiful. We explored the Tower of London, saw the crown jewels, and learned about its famous residents over the centuries including lions, tigers, and bears!

Saturday dawned with a "shakeout run" to loosen up the legs and muscles. I ran through St. James's Park and around the "Birdcage Walk," a street that runs from Horse Guards Road to the Buckingham gate. King James named it after the aviary of exotic birds on that same street. I ran all the way to the finish line area directly in front of Buckingham Palace. The finish line looked stunning, decorated with British flags and vibrant flowers everywhere.

The night before the race, Pam, our husbands, and I gathered for a carb-loading dinner. We vibrated with excitement, chatting about the race, what we thought would happen, and the sights we hoped to see. Because the London streets were narrow and there would be over fifty thousand runners, the organizers had created several start lines that were color-coded. Pam and I weren't in the same start line and wouldn't see each other at the beginning of the race. Knowing we wouldn't meet again until after the race, we said our goodbyes and wished each other luck.

Race day arrived. I had trained in all types of weather and endured the pain, sacrifice, and the highs and lows that come with weeks of preparation. With my start time set for 10:00 a.m., I ate breakfast at the hotel, grabbed a banana and bottled water, then boarded the Marathon Tours bus. We drove what seemed like a long way, twenty-six miles, in fact. As we made our way to the start, I reflected on all my training. The long runs, the track sessions, the tempo workouts, and the twenty-three-miler with all the wrong turns. I thought about all the "firsts" I had achieved. *Was I ready? Could I really do this?*

As we arrived in Blackheath, Southeast London, we stepped off the bus onto what looked like a giant soccer field. Tents were set up with heaters serving tea and coffee. Large projection screens captured the elite runners lining up to begin the race, adding to the electric atmosphere.

The first thing on my agenda finding a porta-john quickly took an unexpected turn. Instead, I stumbled upon a "women's area" where I received an oddly shaped, elongated cardboard contraption. I rounded the corner and saw a line of women with their pants down, all wielding this strange device, attempting to pee while standing up. Of course, I had never seen so many naked butts in one place, and I stood there, completely flabbergasted, trying to figure out how to use this foreign instrument (which I later learned was a female urinal). In that moment, I thought if only I could find a bathroom that didn't require an engineering degree. *No porta-johns? How does anyone go number two in this setup?* I fumbled with the female urinal but gave up in defeat, my efforts as futile as trying to fold a fitted sheet. As I walked out, I spotted a massive trash can overflowing with the discarded cardboard devices. Eww! And then, a long row of porta-johns, which I never imagined I'd be so relieved to see. Thank you, God!

I took refuge in the tea tent, hoping to keep warm, but the smell of body odor hit me like an unwanted wave crashing into my nostrils. I covered my nose and quickly retreated into the fresh, cold air. It was a delightful, drizzly, forty-degree day, perfect for running.

Soon, my corral was called, and we began to line up. Shivering in my throwaway clothes, I tried to keep warm by doing squats and chatting with the women around me. One woman had trained all winter in Glasgow, Scotland, where the sun didn't rise until mid-morning, and the sky grew dark by mid-afternoon. She had trained alone in all that freezing cold. I admired her fortitude. As I looked around, doubts crept in. *Could I do this? Could I go the distance? What if I needed to stop?* But, just as quickly, I pushed those thoughts aside and focused on the sea of colorful, outrageous costumes. People were not just running a marathon they were in full-on fancy dress, each outfit more bizarre than the last. I couldn't help but laugh as a man in a Superman suit zoomed by, his cape flapping wildly in the wind, while a group of people ran in giant, inflatable bananas, bouncing along the pavement. A woman dressed as a giant pink flamingo waddled past, flapping her feathered arms for balance. It was impossible not to smile at the ridiculousness, and it hit me these people weren't just running for a time; they were running for fun, aiming for a Guinness World Record for the most outrageous costumes. The energy was infectious, and I couldn't help but feel swept up in the madness of it all.

I had trained for the marathon using the Galloway Run-Walk-Run method, developed by American Olympian Jeff Galloway. His approach aimed to prevent injuries during long races by incorporating planned walk breaks. After doing my research, I found it worked well for me in training, so I decided to stick with it for the race. My strategy was simple: run for nine minutes, then power walk for one minute. The walking breaks helped lower my heart rate and conserve energy, keeping me strong throughout the race.

As our corral moved forward, the race had already been underway for twenty or thirty minutes. I anticipated a surge of energy or fanfare, but once the gun went off, we were simply running. I felt a little self-conscious walking during that first mile, especially as the crowd cheered us on, but I stuck to my plan despite the urge to push harder.

As I ran, I spotted loads of people (mostly men) darting off the course to pee along a fence line or behind a car. There were portable stalls where men could just run up and relieve themselves. Must be nice to have it so easy. I needed to pee from the start. Each time I passed a porta-john, a line of people waited. I pressed on, but by the time I hit the 10K mark, I couldn't hold it any longer and stopped at a "portaloo," the British version of a porta-john.

Fortunately, only one person stood ahead of me, so I figured it would be quick. But as I waited, impatience crept in. I started knocking on the door, urging them to "hurry up" and reminding them, "We're in a race here!" I even added a cheerful, "Come on, we can do this!" The poor soul eventually emerged, looking like they'd just escaped a hostage situation.

I could almost hear them muttering under their breath about "rude, pushy Americans."

The first part of the race felt like I was weaving through a series of "hamlets" with colorful, ethnic neighborhoods, each with its own unique flair. Families gathered to cheer us on, toddlers in strollers waved enthusiastically, and kids stretched out their hands for high-fives while half-drunk patrons hung out of the pubs, giving us all the encouragement they could muster, which was sometimes a bit slurred.

At one point, I found myself running alongside a man carrying a cross, sporting a crown of thorns on his head, and wearing a loincloth that barely covered his dignity. Oh, and he was barefoot. Naturally, the spectators went wild, calling out everything from "Go Jesus!" to "You're amazing, Jesus!" and "Jesus H. Christ!" I've never heard so many variations of this name in my life. For a few miles, we ran side by side, and while the initial comments were hilarious, they started to wear thin. I picked up my pace, trying to distance myself from the divine spectacle, but I had to give props to Jesus for carrying that cross and running barefoot for 26.2 miles.

London played weather roulette, offering us rain, sleet, snow, hail, and then, just for fun, a little sunshine. I had opted for a long-sleeve thermal top under my "marathon" T-shirt (a creative polyglot with the word "marathon" in five different languages). I completed the ensemble with cropped leggings, gloves (a tactical decision since I wasn't about to toss those this time), a ball cap, and my trusty hydration vest.

As we ran through water stations, water bottles were flying everywhere like confetti at a parade. Runners would take a few sips of an eight-ounce bottle and then toss it aside like they were hot potatoes. I couldn't believe how many perfectly good bottles ended up littering the course, which looked like a plastic landfill in the making. It was both impressive and concerning; I felt like I was running through an eco-disaster movie. At that moment, I was trying not to slip on a bottle and go down.

As I reached the halfway point on the iconic Tower Bridge, the energy amped up a few thousand watts. Fans stood six to eight deep, screaming and cheering as if we were rock stars. I had planned for Scott to meet me near this spot, but, as fate would have it, neither of us saw the other. Unbeknownst to me, he had embarked on a wild Tube adventure, zipping around London in a desperate attempt to catch a glimpse of his running wife. Later, he would lament that running made for the worst spectator sport ever. The poor guy probably ended up more exhausted than I did by the end.

I stuck to my 9:1 run/walk ratio and felt great as I posed for cameras at major landmarks, grinning like I was in a photoshoot. But then came the dreaded out-and-back section around mile seventeen or eighteen, which hit me harder than a Monday morning without caffeine. Many runners dread out-and-back routes since we would see the same scenery going both ways. Plus, the mind game of waiting for the turn to head back the way we just came added to the struggle. During training, eighteen miles became my archnemesis. I could tackle twenty miles like a champ, but eighteen? That felt like a bad breakup.

As I pushed through, I spotted the faster runners nearing the end of the out-and-back section, which gave me a much-needed boost. They were picking up the pace as they neared the finish, and I couldn't wait to be where they were. After we powered through the out-and-back area, we ran under a long overpass so enclosed it felt like a tunnel where eight to ten people had gathered, pounding on huge drums. It was electric! The deep, rhythmic beats reverberated through my chest, fueling my legs with a surge of adrenaline. With only three or four miles to go, I ditched my 9:1 ratio and began running.

I powered through the final 5K, pushing harder than I thought possible, my pace faster than any of my previous splits. As I rounded Big Ben and the Birdcage, Buckingham Palace loomed ahead, and my body screamed for relief. The crowds were a sea of faces, massive and deafening, their cheers urging me on and giving me much-needed strength. I knew Scott was somewhere in that throng, but I couldn't spot him through the commotion.

Then came the signs: eight hundred meters to go, four hundred, and finally two hundred. Each one felt like a countdown to something monumental. As I closed in on the finish line, the energy surged through me an electric force that made my heart race. Everywhere I looked, runners raised their fingers in triumphant victory, and without thinking, I joined in, a grin spreading across my face, ear to ear. This marked the moment the culmination of every step, every sacrifice.

I crossed the finish line of my first-ever marathon in 4:42:45, and a rush of emotions flooded me; elation, pride, disbelief, and pure uncontainable joy. I never imagined I'd run a marathon, let alone run in a city as legendary as London. In that moment, I realized it: I had become a marathoner.

I grabbed my finisher T-shirt, wrapped myself in a mylar sheet for warmth, and headed toward the family meet-and-greet area inside St. James's Park. The crowd was overwhelming; each step felt like a push against a sea of bodies. I had caught a glimpse of a sign that said, "International Runners This Way," but I ignored it, trusting that Scott and I had planned to meet at the "G" sign in the family area. He had my change of clothes, water, nutrition, and, most importantly, a warm hug.

But when I reached the spot, no Scott. I waited. And waited. Minutes stretched into what felt like hours. A chill crept into my bones as the sweat on my skin cooled in the forty-degree air. The cramps in my legs worsened, and the exhaustion from the race began to settle deep in my muscles. I tried to stay composed, but tears welled up. Why wasn't he here?

The park was a labyrinth of faces, and I wondered if he had gotten lost in the chaos. I sank down onto the curb, the weight of the moment crashing down on me, and allowed the tears to spill. *Where was he?*

It soon dawned on me to pull out my phone. It was flooded with calls and texts from him, each one more frantic than the last. He had been trying to get into the park but couldn't. I needed to come to him.

"I can't get in the park. You have to come to me," he said when I called him.

"How come?"

"I can't cross the course," he said impatiently. "You have to come to me."

I didn't realize the course was cantilevered designed so families and spectators could cross without disrupting the runners. But crossing proved challenging. With thousands of runners still pounding the pavement, the process took time. I started to shiver uncontrollably. I tried to keep it together, but the tears came harder. The kindness of strangers never ceased to amaze me as they let me cut in line and helped me shuffle closer to the front. Forty-five minutes after crossing the finish line, I spotted him.

I broke down, crying hysterically, my body shaking with the cold and the release of tension. I couldn't stop. We had been married for twenty years, and in all that time, Scott had only seen me cry on a handful of occasions. He had never witnessed me break down like this. His voice filled with concern.

"Are you hurt? Did you fall? Are you bleeding? Did you sprain your ankle? Do you need to go to the hospital?" I laughed through my tears, the sound shaky but genuine.

"I'm fine," I told him. "I just need a hot bath, food, and to lie down." Without another word, he wrapped me in his arms, bundled me up, and we made our way back to the hotel. Once there, he pampered me with a hot Epsom salt bath, snacks, and the quiet comfort of being in his care.

If I had read the directions in the runner's guide, I would have paid attention to the "International Runners" sign, which would have spared me the mess at St. James's Park and the madness of crossing the course by going the other way out. Instead, I unknowingly subjected myself to a shivering ordeal that felt like a scene from a survival movie.

After a solid rest and soak, we met up with Pam and her husband for post-race beer and dinner in the West End. Pam also had a fantastic time and loved the race. We took photos of our medals and our coveted finisher jackets while we talked nonstop about our day, including the funny signs, costumes, neighborhoods, and sights and sounds. Later, I would find out that I had been the 988,545[th] runner to cross the finish line just 11,455 away from being the millionth finisher. I was proud to have run the London Marathon.

After a while, we said goodbye to Pam and Tom. They were headed back to the States the next day while Scott and I were traveling on to Scotland for a few days.

Before I knew it, we were back in Wilmington, still basking in the post-marathon glow. I decided to take two weeks off running to let my tendons and ligaments recover. It was a nice break to do something other than run. I biked, walked, and enjoyed reconnecting with friends I had neglected during my training.

As much as I enjoyed the time away, the siren calls of running began to pull me back. Yet, something inside me struggled. After conquering one of the world's most incredible marathons and following it up with a fabulous trip to Scotland, how could I possibly top that?

Just when I thought I had life figured out, the ground beneath me shattered. Everything I had known crumbled into turmoil. In that whirlwind, running became my lifeline and desperate escape from the storm. It wasn't just a coping mechanism anymore; it became my battle cry.

A fierce reminder that even in the darkest of times, I could find strength in the rhythm of my breath and the pounding of my feet.

London Marathon, April 24, 2016

Chapter 5 – Runner Highs and Lows

Have you ever experienced euphoria? That state where everything feels lighter, brighter, and blissful? I found it the moment breath control clicked into place on easy runs. Running without gasping for air became the true essence of the sport. But the real magic happened when I could maintain breath control in a group that's when the talking started.

Conversations flowed effortlessly. Ever notice how talking to teenagers in the car feels easier when you're driving, looking ahead rather than at each other?

It's the same with running. Something about moving side by side, in rhythm, made conversations feel deeper. Small talk quickly gave way to more personal topics digestive struggles, bodily functions, life's messier details. Within minutes, I'd find myself sharing things with people I'd just met as if it were the most natural conversation in the world. The running community had its own brand of honesty unfiltered, raw, and occasionally graphic. I often get asked how I can run without throwing up, pooping my pants, or otherwise having gastrointestinal disasters. The truth? I did! When I first started running, 5K races were my jam. Three miles seemed totally manageable until I realized they're basically long, torturous sprints that can lead to some unfortunate bodily fluid releases.

One hot day in May, I decided to tackle a local 5K, fueled by the desire to snag an age-group award. Why? The prize was a Freaker. A one-size-fits-all koozie. This local gem, created in 2011 by the eccentric artist Zach Crain, used recycled sweaters to make a colorful sock with funny images and sayings. Even with millions sold around the world and many readily available in local stores, I wanted to win *that* Freaker. Whether or not it meant risking heat stroke and a potential emergency room visit.

From start to finish, the sun beat down on us. The hot and humid air made it hard to breathe. Little kids would zip past me, their arms and legs flailing wildly, but quickly run out of steam and start walking a quarter mile later. Meanwhile, as the oppressive heat smothered me, my heart hammering in my chest, my lungs feeling heavy and tight, my stomach churning and sloshing, I pushed on, running with every last ounce of energy.

When the finish line came into view, a rush of relief flooded me. I crossed the line and celebrated my victory by promptly throwing up on a volunteer's shoes. Embarrassed, apologetic, and despite the mess, I had done it, I had won that Freaker.

I often get asked how I manage to run in the heat. Well, the truth is, I'm absolutely terrible at it. I'll never understand how some runners can maintain their pace regardless of temperatures, whether a stifling ninety degrees or a cool fifty. I am definitely not one of those magical creatures. For me, heat means slower speeds, gastrointestinal distress, and a chorus of complaints that could rival any symphony.

After London, I struggled to find motivation. Sure, I ran with my newfound tribe, but my log entries read like a sad teenage diary: "Didn't feel it today." "Whole body hurt." "It was hot." I logged more complaints than actual mileage. Welcome to the "marathon blues," where the struggle bus stops often, and the lack of enthusiasm prevails.

Many runners experience "the blues" after a big race or major accomplishment. Rightfully so, the training and preparation consumed days, weeks, and months of our lives. Once race day arrived and the culmination of the day finished, there was a post-race letdown, often accompanied by feelings of emptiness, fatigue, and loss of purpose.

It took a solid four months to find my next goal. I zeroed in on obtaining a personal record (PR) in the Half Marathon. I had a number of half marathons under my belt, but they were all sort of a mess. I had calf cramps in one; I struggled and almost collapsed in another. I wanted to run a personal best and run it "right," which meant doing a negative split where I would run the second half faster than the first half and feel good enough at the end to leave everything I had on the course. It also meant I wanted to run the race in under two hours.

My running friends and I sought out fun racing venues. We settled on the Richmond, Virginia, Half Marathon, dubbed "The Friendliest Race in America" in November 2016. This race offered both full and half marathon distances, so several members of the tribe opted for the full, while most of us stuck to the half. We split up, reserved hotel rooms, and kicked off the training cycle.

During my workouts, I focused on training for speed and strength. When I wasn't at the track running sprints or the gym lifting weights, I was out running tempo runs, which helped train my body for a fast finish. I'd like to say I drastically changed my diet and stopped drinking wine, beer, and Grey Goose, but I didn't. I did cut back a lot during training, but Friday nights in Wilmington exploded with live music, social gatherings, and fun times; I always planned my long runs around my FOMO.

As I trained in the blistering heat of the summer, I found myself constantly battling GI distress, along with the all-too-familiar mad dash to the bathroom that seemed to come out of nowhere. Every long run felt like an uphill struggle, my body rebelling against the intense humidity and the constant discomfort. But through it all, I kept reminding myself that fall was just around the corner.

The thought of crisp, cool mornings kept me going. Soon, I'd be running in the kind of weather where the air felt refreshing and energizing instead of suffocating. Autumn would bring the perfect conditions no more sweating through every mile or dealing with stomach issues triggered by heat. The cool, invigorating breeze would make each step feel lighter, each mile a little less grueling.

Until then, I endured the summer struggles, focusing on the bigger picture. I knew that if I could push through this unrelenting heat, the rewards would come when the weather finally turned. It felt like a long wait, but the promise of cooler, more comfortable runs kept my spirits up and my legs moving.

The Richmond Half Marathon arrived at the perfect time for a fast race with cool November temperatures and a stunning finish along the James River. Adding to the celebratory vibe of that beautiful final stretch, was the thrilling downhill finish flanked by craft beer vendors. The race offered excellent swag, including a shirt, hat, and my favorite: a cozy blanket.

Race day arrived cold, hovering in the mid-thirties, and despite the chill, I overdid it with layers. Annoyed, I shed clothes during the race and wrapped them around my waist, which didn't make for cute race photos.

I started conservatively, planning to run the first three miles at a ten-minute pace per mile and gradually pick up speed each mile. By mile eleven, I planned to give myself permission to let loose and run as fast as I could.

The entire race felt amazing. I executed my strategy flawlessly, and if anything, I may have sandbagged too much at the start. When I reached mile eleven, I flipped the switch. I pushed hard and entered a flow state, running faster than ever through downtown Richmond. Turning the corner, I smiled all the way down the big hill toward the finish line. I crossed the line feeling like I could easily run another three miles. Ecstatic, I rang the PR bell (loudly) and beamed with a smile that lasted all day. The race was perfection, and to this day, the Richmond Half Marathon still holds my personal record. I hit my sub-two-hour goal with a time of 1:58 arms in the air, smile wide, practically an entire wardrobe wrapped around my waist.

After my PR at Richmond, my confidence soared, and I decided to take on the Chicago Marathon. It hadn't been on my radar, not a glimmer, not a flicker. But that PR lit a fire under me like a flaming slice of deep-dish pizza. I felt like I knew how to run a marathon and could do it again. After missing the lottery deadline, I threw my name in the hat to run for a charity. I had never raised a dime for anything, nor did I have the faintest idea how to go about it, but the charity's website promised plenty of resources, which I took as either a hopeful sign or, at the very least, an invitation to learn something new.

After a few back-and-forth emails that made me feel like I was signing my life away, I committed to raising $3,000. And by "committed" I mean I signed up for a financial game of "Will I or won't I?" If I didn't raise the money, I'd be footing the bill myself. Thankfully, I would be running for a great cause, Homes for Our Troops. They built adaptive housing for severely disabled post-9/11 vets. The mission of Homes for Our Troops resonated with me and gave me confidence and belief I could raise the funds.

The Chicago Marathon took place in October 2017, which meant I was facing summer training sessions that could easily be renamed "Barfing, Pooping, and Heat Distress: A Summer of Misery." Sure, I had trained for half marathons in the sweltering heat before, but a full marathon? I had no idea the mental and physical toll it would take to train in ninety degrees and higher temperatures. Like an unrelenting sauna, the heat and humidity in coastal North Carolina never quits.

As I fixated on this shiny new goal, everything changed in an instant. The next journey I embarked on challenged my resolve and shook me to my core. It tested my strength. Every step felt like a battle, each one more difficult than the last, yet somehow, I had to keep moving forward, unable to turn back.

On June 19, 2017, our world was shattered when Scott received a cancer diagnosis. We stood paralyzed, consumed by shock. If you've ever faced something like this, you know the gut-wrenching jolt it delivers to your very core. We were young, healthy, and vibrant. We exercised regularly. We were committed to a life of wellness. In our minds, cancer was something that happened to other people.

A few months earlier, while shaving, Scott noticed a lump on the side of his neck. At first, he brushed it off, dismissing it as nothing. But during a visit to his parents, his stepmother's concerned words echoed in his mind. "You need to get that checked out," she'd said. He promised her he would and made an appointment with his primary care doctor, who offered the questionable advice to simply "watch it." In hindsight, that advice proved to be a grave mistake. A large lump on the neck isn't normal, it's a red flag.

As we waited, helplessly watching, the lump grew larger, a ticking time bomb we couldn't defuse. Within thirty days, it became unmistakably bigger, prompting his doctor to order a biopsy, but by then, the damage had already been done.

All along, we had convinced ourselves it was some sort of allergy, a benign issue near his lymph nodes. He exercised regularly, ate a balanced diet, and looked like the picture of health. None of that mattered when the biopsy results came back, the word "malignant" echoing in our minds like a death knell. When the doctor broke the news, he casually mentioned the possibility of "head or neck cancer." In that moment, we felt like characters in a horror film, where the worst-case scenarios are tossed around with no regard for the gravity of the situation. I'll never forget the look on Scott's face when he walked through the door to tell me the diagnosis. We were enveloped in disbelief, tears streaming down our faces.

"Cancer" is such a heavy word, and when paired with "head and neck," it felt like a sentence of doom. My thoughts spiraled into the darkest corners of my mind. *Could he have brain cancer?* I could not fathom a world where Scott had cancer. *How could this happen?* I couldn't get my mind wrapped around the idea. In that moment, our lives shifted, and the battle for clarity and strength had only just begun.

The radiologist recommended an ear, nose, and throat (ENT) doctor. Moments after the examination, the doctor diagnosed Scott with "base of tongue cancer," essentially throat cancer. Our minds raced at full speed. Despite the doctor's warning not to Google anything, we immediately began searching. Scott had already struggled with swallowing due to the lump on his neck, making it terrifying to consider the tumor as the cause.

The first priority was a CT scan to determine the size and location of the tumor. I often described the following weeks as "getting on the cancer train." After the diagnosis, it felt like stepping into a busy car dealership each doctor pushing their plan, eager to lock us into their system, which allowed no time or space for research or exploring alternatives. They dismissed the idea of non-traditional treatments. We found ourselves juggling appointments with oncologists, radiologists, and a parade of specialists. Cancer terrified us, and the medical professionals seemed all too aware of how to exploit that fear to keep the money flowing into their system.

The ENT told us to expect a grueling treatment, one of the toughest protocols out there. Because of the tumor's location and its potential to affect breathing, swallowing, and eating, Scott had received a stage 4 throat cancer diagnosis. Despite the heavy news, a glimmer of hope remained: the five-year survival rate exceeded 90 percent as long as we stuck to the treatment plan. Everything came to a halt as chemotherapy and radiation loomed ahead. We canceled vacation and work trips, and I dove into research about throat cancer and cancer in general, trying to grasp what we were up against.

Scott's cancer stemmed from the Human Papillomavirus (HPV), a virus that can lie dormant in the body for years. I came to learn that many cancers are caused by viruses, far more often than by genetic predispositions. Unfortunately, Scott became one of the unlucky ones. For men, HPV-related cancer often presents in the throat. The flood of information was inundating, but I needed to absorb as much knowledge as possible to support him through this.

The treatment protocol included thirty-five rounds of radiation and seven rounds of chemo. The chemo drug, Cisplatin, was labeled "light," and meant Scott wouldn't lose his hair or endure extreme illness we were thankful for small mercies. But let's be real: it was still chemo. While the chemical structure differed, it was still derived from mustard gas. The idea that this toxic substance could somehow "heal" patients baffled me. I couldn't help but feel a deep, secret horror as I watched the bags of Cisplatin drip into Scott's arm at the treatment center. I didn't want to expose Scott to my true feelings, so I put on a brave face, offering him support, while inside, I couldn't help but think, *There has to be a better way to cure cancer.*

And then came radiation. That proved no picnic either. Scott had to be fitted with a metal cage that clamped tightly around his face, then bolted to a table while the radiation machine circled his head, zapping the tumor into oblivion. The process didn't just target the cancer it also wreaked havoc on his skin, mouth, teeth, and throat, leaving a trail of damage in its wake.

Once treatment began, Scott's health took a sharp decline. He often felt sick after chemo, and the daily radiation sessions wore him down. The pain became debilitating, and eating was a constant struggle. He lost pounds rapidly, starving but unable to eat due to the pain. I found myself eating away from home, just so he wouldn't have to see or smell what I ate.

Our social life vanished, replaced only by the nurses and doctors we saw daily. It turned into an incredibly lonely time for both of us. Running became my refuge, my way of coping with the insanity surrounding us. Scott endured constant pain, struggled to swallow, and eventually relied on a feeding tube for nutrition. The prescribed pain meds Fentanyl mixed with Oxycontin hit hard, leaving him in a haze. He often fell asleep in the most random places like while trying to tie his shoes, strumming his guitar, or, in one particularly memorable moment, leaning against the car and dozing off while standing up.

I recall Labor Day Weekend, a time when we'd usually be barbecuing, hitting the beach, or enjoying outdoor concerts. Instead, Scott slept on the couch, and I scrambled to find ways to occupy my time. I spent an entire day trimming our Jasmine vine, which had grown wild and out of control. The simple act of cutting branches and stripping away the overgrowth brought me a small measure of peace, a momentary escape from the heaviness of everything else. I kept running and training, clinging to the sanity that came from lacing up my shoes and hitting the pavement as my once-strong, healthy husband dwindled down to 150 pounds on his 6'2" frame. It tore me up inside.

To make matters worse, I developed plantar fasciitis during this stressful time. This unbearable pain in my right foot forced me to take breaks from running. Inflammation on the thick band of tissue that runs from your heel to your toes can cause horrific pain for runners. I've heard runners say that running will break your heart, and in this case, it was true. My running tribe continued on without me, and I felt like a ghost watching from the sidelines. I missed those conversations we had while we pounded the pavement together, and it stung to feel left out.

I remember one morning being left behind as my friends ran ahead, unaware of my absence. I didn't blame them; they focused on their goals, their paces, and keeping the group together. But the experience hurt both mentally and physically. To heal, I had to accept that I needed to slow down, even if it meant stepping away from the camaraderie that once lifted me up.

Scott finished his last rounds of treatment in mid-September, and I focused on getting him healthy as quickly as possible. Slowly, the stress and emotional weight of cancer treatment began to lift. For months, I had juggled summer training in the sweltering heat, cared for him, battled plantar fasciitis, raised money for my charity, and worked full-time. The mix of sadness, guilt, and confusion had been draining, but through it all, Scott kept encouraging me to run the race. He never wanted me to give up my goals or dreams.

I didn't expect to enjoy fundraising for the race. Working with a charity that had such a strong mission made all the difference. Thanks to the generosity of my friends and family, I ended up being one of the top three fundraisers. They showered me with some great swag, pre- and post-race hospitality, and lots of well wishes. Homes for Our Troops turned out to be an incredible organization doing vital work for our post-9/11 vets, and I couldn't have been prouder to wear their jersey in the race.

After a summer of training through injuries and the stress of Scott's treatment, I became determined to run. I craved a break, an escape, and by race day, Scott had weaned off the strong meds and could fend for himself. Emerging from a fog, I felt ready to embrace the thrill and energy of the race and the support of the running community.

Runners often get sick when they start tapering and reducing mileage before a marathon due to a suppressed immune system from all the training, and I proved no exception. A sore throat hit the week before the race, and on top of that, my plantar fasciitis screamed at me. Add to that the guilt of leaving my sick husband for a long weekend, and the weight of it all felt enormous. Looking back, I realized I should have cut myself some slack and been kinder. My logbook read like a sad country song: "Foot pain, pain, pain, and more pain." A recurring theme.

Despite everything, I repeatedly woke up at 4:00 a.m. and ran in the pre-dawn hours on the dark streets of Wilmington while I listened to true crime podcasts. I pounded the pavement by myself and developed a crust of grit that I'd never had before. I finished my last long run and wrote in my log, "I'm ready to kill it!" I was ready to tackle whatever the race threw at me, even if I felt like I was running on fumes.

I packed a bag, hugged Scott goodbye, and boarded the plane for Chicago, confident I had the marathon under control. I knew what to expect and how to run the distance.

Chapter 6 – Chicago Marathon 2017

O ctober 8, 2017, marked the fortieth running of the Chicago Marathon, and as I touched down in the city, anticipation surged through me. I'd always loved Chicago for its stunning architecture, mouthwatering food, and that charming Midwestern vibe. My Indonesian friend Rina and I booked a fantastic hotel near the start and finish lines, which made logistics a breeze.

After arriving, we dropped our bags and headed straight to McCormick Place, just south of downtown, for the expo. Unlike London, the Chicago expo felt like a runner's paradise. Marathon legends shared their wisdom on stage, we sifted through racks of stylish athletic wear, and an abundance of race swag awaited us.

I indulged and picked up T-shirts, a cozy hoodie, and a finisher jacket. We snapped tons of photos at the expo showing the marathon route and gawked at the World Marathon Majors booth, which showcased the coveted Six Star Medal in a glass case. Before London and meeting Pam,

I hadn't heard of the World Marathon Majors or the Six Star Medal. "The Majors" included six races: London, Chicago, Berlin, Boston, New York City, and Tokyo. Pharmaceutical company Abbott Laboratories had started sponsoring the World Majors years earlier and created a platform to help runners begin their Six Star journey. No special prerequisites existed to start, runners simply had to create a profile in the portal and, as they completed races, add their finish times. It seemed easy enough, except, of course, the real challenge lay in securing an entry and, above all, running the marathons.

The thought of running six marathons and earning the Six Star Medal seemed an enormous task I wasn't sure I could take on. *Could I really run six marathons?* The idea felt kind of impossible, but after having finished one marathon, my confidence started to grow. The adventure began to feel within reach, yet still, it seemed like an epic goal far beyond my capabilities. Once I saw that Six Star Medal on display, however, something ignited within me.

The next morning, we did a quick shakeout around our hotel, which took us through the beautiful sights of Millennium Park. The city vibrated with energy like it had downed a double shot of espresso. We decided to save our legs and hop on an architectural riverboat tour to see all the gorgeous sights of downtown Chicago. After our architectural immersion, we headed over to Navy Pier, where we rode the Centennial Wheel on a surprisingly windy day. Let's just say it was a real test of my core strength and my ability to keep my lunch down. It was also oddly warm for October in Chicago, which made me wonder if I accidentally signed up for a summer marathon.

Race day dawned bright and bustling. After a couple of days playing tourist in Chicago, we were ready to lace up our running shoes and hit the pavement. Rina and I were pumped to tackle the fast, flat course. The staff at the Residence Inn on LaSalle Street were absolute gems, setting out bagels and bananas for the marathoners. With breakfast in hand, we made our way to the start line on foot. We both preferred to arrive early, which was perfect for visiting the porta-johns four times and ensuring we had ample time to find our corral. After navigating security, dodging crowds, and waiting in line for the bathrooms three more times, we finally settled into our corral, jittery with anticipation.

As we mingled with fellow runners, the excitement in the air was undeniable. The Chicago Marathon kicks off at Grant Park, where the starting line is divided into multiple corrals, labeled A through I, based on the number of participants.

Corrals were assigned according to your qualifying time or expected pace, with the fastest runners in the first few. To keep things moving smoothly, corrals released every few minutes, easing congestion like a well-oiled machine. Someone belted out the Star-Spangled Banner, and we all readied ourselves, watches in hand, mentally preparing for the journey ahead. Veterans of the race had warned me about the GPS shenanigans in downtown Chicago, thanks to the towering skyscrapers; they made it clear I'd need to run by feel at the start and not obsess over my pace. It had been a long road to get here, and I was determined to soak in the excitement and enjoy the moment.

A crisp chill lingered in the air, but the blue sky promised a perfect day in downtown Chicago. The energy radiated, and everyone seemed fired up, ready to crush the race. When the gun went off, it felt like the starting pistol for pure excitement. Slowly, our wave moved toward the timing mat. We pressed "start" on our watches, and just like that, marathon number two officially kicked off.

This time, no doubts clouded my mind. I embraced the run, determined to savor every moment the sights, the sounds, the roar of the crowds without the pressure of a finish time. Yet, a secret goal still lingered in the back of my mind, a quiet challenge I couldn't shake. I wanted to run faster than London just for the sake of running faster. Something every runner has probably thought but can't explain why.

As I ran past a nursing home, I saw residents waving from their windows, their smiles bright and full of life. In that moment, a wave of emotion swept over me. I felt an overwhelming sense of gratitude, as though the universe itself had placed me there at that exact time to witness something profound. Tears welled up as cheers rang in my ears, a powerful reminder that this race, this day, and this journey were nothing short of extraordinary.

The morning felt perfectly invigorating. I hummed along strong and free, sticking to my run/walk strategy and maintaining a steady 10:30 pace per mile. Timing mats intersected the course at 5K intervals, tracking each runner's progress and capturing their "chip time." Each runner wore a chip inside the race bib, which registered their time when crossing the mats. This system helped organizers ensure everyone passed each timing point and allowed fans to track their athletes in real-time using a phone app. As I crossed the 5K mats, I blew kisses to the sky, knowing Scott and my family were tracking and cheering me from afar.

As the miles wore on, the sun began to beat down, but I maintained my focus. The crowds boosted me, their cheers blending with the dynamic energy of the course, and the scenery entertained me. There were Elvis impersonators, drag queens in Boystown, and colorful dragons in Chinatown. I made sure to fuel up as needed, staying hydrated and nourished.

Around the halfway point, I saw my friend Rina. She looked like she was having a rough time and confessed that this race wasn't going well for her. She decided to run with me for the rest of the way. While I was glad to have her company, I couldn't help but notice that her struggles seemed to affect my own energy. As she expressed her frustration and disappointment, I felt a shift in the atmosphere. What started as a shared experience began to feel heavier, and I found myself absorbing some of her negativity. It wasn't that I didn't want to support her but I could sense that her frustration was slowly draining my own enthusiasm, making the journey feel a little more challenging than it had been before.

As we made our way through the South Side of Chicago, a knot of anxiety twisted in my stomach. The area had a reputation, and though I tried not to dwell on it, I couldn't shake the unease. Thankfully, we passed through without incident, but the rising temperature only added to my discomfort.

At mile seventeen, a row of porta-johns came into view, but not surprisingly, they were surrounded by a long line of runners. I leaned toward Rina and whispered urgently, "I really need to go. I can't wait."

"What should we do?" she asked.

"Distract them," I said.

Without hesitation, she sprang into action. Her Indonesian charm came alive as she pretended not to speak English very well. She launched into a conversation about the race, the scorching heat, and how her friend (me!) was in desperate need of relief.

All eyes turned to her. I didn't know what she was saying, but it didn't matter. It worked. While everyone's attention was focused on Rina, I snuck into the porta-john, grateful for my friend's quick thinking and impeccable timing. I didn't want to be a statistic, especially that kind of statistic. With her comedic brilliance keeping the crowd entertained, I made my escape into the porta-john just in the nick of time. I emerged without making eye contact with anyone in the now curious line and rejoined Rina on the course; I felt like a ninja who had completed a stealth mission.

We laughed and ran/walked until we hit Michigan Avenue, known as the "Miracle Mile." It felt like that road went on for forty miles, like some sort of running version of Groundhog Day. The finish line was definitely not on Michigan Avenue. There were a couple of turns, and then up the infamous "Mount Roosevelt," which feels like Everest but is actually only a slight incline, and finally, in the distance, we saw the finish line glimmering, taunting us in the bright sun.

By then, my brain had cooked and fried. I experienced that familiar heaviness from London as if my body were throwing a tantrum and refusing to go another step for the last eight hundred meters. At last, crossing the finish line mat with arms raised in victory, I felt a wave of relief wash over me. Maybe I should've had a bigger reaction, like bursting into tears or doing a backflip, but honestly, relief was the overwhelming feeling. It had been a long, winding road to get there, and while my foot held up just enough to finish, it was my stubborn mind that got me through this tough race.

Rina and I collapsed on the sidelines, venting about the heat. She kept repeating to me, "No more maratons. No more maratons," not pronouncing the "th" in marathon. This was coming from a regular at 50K and 50-mile ultra races. I laughed and didn't believe a word of it.

My pace for the last half averaged a sluggish 12:04. As expected, heat was my kryptonite. I felt like I should've performed better, but in hindsight, it's a miracle I even finished with what I consider now to be a "decent" time. As runners, our victories are based on pace and finishing times, which determine how fit we are or how "good" of a runner we are. In reality, it doesn't measure how hard we worked or how dedicated we were to running. I had worked my tail off while juggling work and home-life stress, battling the sweltering temperatures, dealing with dehydration the last half, nursing an injury, and let's not forget, the bathroom break that felt like it took an eternity.

Nevertheless, instead of celebrating, I found myself disappointed with a marathon time of 5:01:01. Rina agreed that anything over five hours felt like a personal failure for both of us. My foot screamed in protest, and the walk back felt like a trek through a war zone. I called Scott as I hobbled down the street to the hotel, tears streaming down my face. My emotions were all over the place. I was happy to have completed my second marathon but disappointed in my time.

I longed for my husband to be there, and combined with the throbbing pain in my foot, it all crashed together.

After literally what felt like a second marathon, we made it back to the hotel. I soaked in Epsom salts while Rina and our other Wilmington friends regaled each other with race stories, laughter bubbling up like the champagne we were about to indulge in. We put our legs up the wall and bonded over the shared agony of what we dubbed "the hottest race ever." Later that evening, we went out for dinner. Despite our disappointing race times, we wore our medals like badges of honor, grinning from ear to ear. After dinner, Rina and I decided to keep the celebration going with a bottle of champagne, still draped in our medals and proudly declaring, "We just ran a marathon!" Eventually we made our way to the popular Cloud Gate, aka "The Bean," in Millennium Park to take photos with our medals, finisher shirts, and jackets. I was grateful for Rina's company. She had a knack for turning my disappointment into laughter.

The next day, we flew home, strutting through the airport with our medals on full display as if they were golden tickets to the coolest club in town. Who needed first class when you could be a marathoner?

Returning home to Scott was a relief. Both of us needed serious healing. We were like two old cars that had just survived a demolition derby battered but still running. I wasn't sure what lay ahead in the marathon world, but I knew my foot required real attention, and Scott needed time to recover from his cancer treatment.

After Chicago, I found myself at a crossroads. With two stars in hand, the Six Star journey beckoned me louder than ever. *Why stop now?* The idea of running through historic cities around the world was too exciting to ignore. It felt like collecting Pokémon, but instead of cute creatures, it was miles, medals, and, admittedly, a whole lot of chafing.

At fifty-one, I made a vow: I would complete the Six Star quest by the time I turned sixty. It seemed a far reach, but deep down, I knew it was about more than just races. Once my mind locked onto a goal, there was no turning back. Trying to stop me now would be like attempting to halt a freight train with a toothpick. My path was set, and there wasn't a force on earth that could derail me. Or so I thought.

Chicago Marathon, October 8, 2017

Chapter 7 – Fully Baked and Well Done

My girlfriends and I decided to take on the Diva Half Marathon in Myrtle Beach in Spring 2018. It's just as fabulous as it sounds. Tiaras, feather boas, tutus, shirtless "firemen" handing out medals, and champagne after the race. It felt like one big celebration wrapped in pink glitter, and my friends and I dove right in. We rented a huge van, had matching shirts made, put on our pink tutus and tiaras, and took off running.

Somewhere along the route, I found myself trailing behind a guy, which struck me as unusual especially in a sea of glittery tutus. But this guy? He clearly had skipped the pre-race porta-john stop and, without a care in the world, wore a pair of poop-filled shorts for the entire thirteen miles. I fought the urge to gag. Around me, the glitter sparkled, and the crowds cheered, but all I could think was, *Why, oh why, do I put myself through these things?* Let's face it, pooping our pants doesn't exactly top anyone's bucket list, but things happen. As mortifying as it seemed, it wasn't much different than projectile vomiting or sweating through your shoes. It all felt equally gross. Scott stood utterly flabbergasted by what I put myself through. I think I saw a healthy dose of horror in his eyes, too. He'd shake his head and call me a "crazy person," which I wore as a badge of honor.

Sometimes, I dreaded telling him about my next wild idea, but he slowly started getting used to my outrageous plans. And honestly, they never seemed all that outrageous to me or to my running friends. To us, it felt like just another Tuesday. Who wouldn't want to run fifteen miles, battling heat, stomach issues, maybe pooping in the bushes? It was all part of the fun, right?

So, while Scott thought I'd lost my marbles, I like to think I collected more stories for the grand adventure of life. This was how I found myself in another summer marathon training cycle for Berlin, this time in the "hot as the gates of hell," known as Southeastern North Carolina.

The Berlin Marathon usually took place in September, just before Oktoberfest kicked off. But in 2018, the race organizers decided to shake things up by moving the race up a week. This meant my training would start in May, right as the weather began its annual transformation into a furnace, ready to turn me into a fried egg on the pavement.

Without telling Scott, I took a leap of faith and entered the lottery with several of my running friends. The lottery was a game of chance, and all you could do was wait for that nail-biting email stating either you're "in," time to celebrate, or you're "out," time to sulk.

Getting an entry into The Majors or Six Star races can be challenging. It's not a matter of going to their website, paying a registration fee, and signing up. Marathons, especially World Marathon Majors, have become very popular and difficult to gain entry. You can obtain entry through time qualifications, lotteries, charities, tour operators, virtual races, or connections if you have any.

Since I wasn't a fast runner, time qualifying for races didn't seem like a viable option. Each marathon had slightly different entry requirements, lottery systems, and odds of gaining an entry. For instance, London had a lottery, but the odds of securing a spot were incredibly low due to the high number of runners seeking entry, and many of its slots were reserved for charity organizations and fundraisers.

Boston stood out as the most notable time qualifier. Unlike most races, it didn't offer a lottery system. Instead, runners could only gain entry by meeting specific qualifying times, raising money for charity, booking through a tour operator (international runners only), or knowing someone who could get them a bib through a corporation or sponsor.

For international runners seeking to run Boston, tour operators offered a potential route to entry, but for U.S. runners, that path didn't exist. While charity slots seemed like an option, they came with their own set of challenges. Charity running had become increasingly competitive as more people entered lotteries and the race for spots got more intense.

Other options for gaining entry were running virtual races and entering mini lotteries. Abbott now offers some race lotteries for runners who hold three or more stars. For the fast runners, gaining entry could be a little easier, provided you have the qualifying time via another marathon. The commitment to run multiple races to qualify can be time-consuming and difficult as well. There is no easy road to the World Majors. It takes effort, time, and money.

The application process for Berlin was a hoot. I had to input my height and weight, and shockingly, they actually considered those details before granting entry. My friend Lori, who was small and petite, accidentally typed in 425 pounds instead of 125 pounds on her form. We all burst into laughter when she told us, but unfortunately, she didn't make the cut. Guess they figured she might need a wider starting line.

Then came my moment of truth: I received the email saying I was "in"! I couldn't believe it. I was over the moon to be part of the forty-fifth running of the Berlin Marathon. Sharing the course with world record holder Eliud Kipchoge felt surreal. With a shot at improving my Chicago time, I couldn't wait to dive into the marathon adventure. The only question now was whether I could survive the training in the heat again.

Scott began his recovery from cancer treatment over a six-month period. I encouraged him to participate in the Livestrong program, which supports cancer patients transitioning back to their normal lives after treatment. Having been on a feeding tube for an extended time, his primary focus was on relearning how to swallow, along with regaining his weight and strength.

He started physical therapy and dedicated himself to improving his swallowing skills. This had always been a challenge for him, even before his cancer diagnosis. We often joked that he was a "choker and gagger" when it came to eating, as he frequently struggled to get food down. Unfortunately, the radiation had damaged his swallowing muscles, and those that weren't damaged had atrophied.

Nevertheless, he persevered with the determination to remove the feeding tube as soon as possible.

"I want to eat and enjoy Thanksgiving dinner," he said. "I don't want to be on the feeding tube anymore."

The holiday was fast approaching, and he wanted to surprise his dad and stepmom with a visit to their home in Delaware. He worked hard on gaining his strength back and being able to make the trip from North Carolina. We also had a trip planned to Malaysia and Thailand in the spring of 2018 through my work, and he wanted to go and be able to enjoy himself without dealing with a feeding tube.

Fortunately, Scott was able to have his feeding tube removed the week before Thanksgiving, which was just in time for some serious turkey action. His swallowing and eating improved, which brought a wonderful sense of normalcy. A few months later, we took the trip to Asia, and it felt like we were reclaiming a piece of our old lives.

We loved exploring new places, hiking, biking, and soaking up the great outdoors. This trip offered all that and more. Although Scott tired out more easily, we had a fantastic time, saw incredible sights, and I ate my weight in delicious food. I even managed to squeeze in some running despite the heat and humidity in Malaysia. One memorable run on the island of

Langkawi featured wild monkeys and colorful birds flitting around like they were auditioning for a nature documentary. It was a run to remember, not just for the sounds but also for the wildlife sightings. We came home from Asia and moved into a new home with less maintenance and upkeep. We had changed a lot in our lives because of Scott's diagnoses. We wanted to make things simpler and easier to enjoy our free time as much as possible.

I'm not going to lie, I was dreading another summer training session and figured it was time to call in the big guns. After reflecting on my Chicago experience, I realized I hadn't fueled properly leading up to the race. Once dehydration hit, coupled with the fact that it had been an unseasonably hot day for Chicago, it felt like I was trying to fill a bathtub with the drain open. I thought, *Why not try to improve my time by bringing in a professional coach with way more experience?* I needed someone who could teach me how to hydrate properly and maybe even remind me that fueling isn't just a suggestion but a requirement.

Listening to a popular podcast about women's running, I absorbed insights from a coach who worked with athletes worldwide. She shared strength and running workouts, along with YouTube videos on foam rolling, stretching, and warm-ups. Everything runners needed to improve. She held "office hours" to discuss workouts or address any running challenges. The idea of having a coach felt foreign. I wasn't focused on running fast or winning, I simply wanted to beat my last marathon time. That 5:01 finish time bruised my ego and lingered like an albatross around my neck. The thought of repeating it in Berlin terrified me. It wasn't just about the time but the effort and dedication I had poured into my training. I needed to prove to myself that I could do better. I wanted my finish time to represent victory, not a painful reminder of a race I'd rather forget.

The idea of running faster danced in my head, Berlin's flat, fast course seemed ideal for it. But after battling plantar fasciitis for the past year, I knew pushing myself further would only lead to injury. My speed sessions had become speed traps, and my mileage had crept to the point where my body sent clear signals to stop.

A long, serious conversation with myself revealed that I wasn't as smart as I'd thought. My running group hit paces I couldn't sustain without risking injury. I reminded myself that they would still be my friends, even if we didn't run together. That turned out to be true, though some of them moved on faster than my quickest mile. Yes, it hurt, and yes, it stung. But deep down, I knew I wanted to run without pain more.

After meeting with my new coach, she suggested heart rate training. It felt revolutionary to trade my pursuit of speed for a more sustainable approach. It was time to rediscover the joy of running, one heartbeat at a time. The concept behind heart rate training was simple: run easy runs with a low heart rate to become more efficient. During speed or tempo work, my heart rate would naturally rise, increasing my exertion. Most marathon training should be done in heart rate zones two or three, which usually correspond to a range of around 130–140 beats per minute. While we didn't get into a scientific deep dive into heart rate training, there were other factors to consider, like sleep, diet, caffeine intake, and stress. I explored plenty of information on the internet and geeked out on the specifics and benefits. I wanted to try to change the way I trained to avoid being injured.

The first step? Slowing down to about a twelve-minute mile pace to keep my heart rate below 140. It felt like crawling and maintaining good form at that speed was awkward and unnatural. Luckily, I began this process during a rare snow and ice storm in our town. The roads became treacherous, forcing me to slow down whether I liked it or not. It seemed like the universe's way of saying, "Leave your ego at the door and just run a twelve-minute mile." Honestly, after battling plantar fasciitis and taking months off from running, I was more than grateful to be back on my feet, even if it meant moving at a turtle's pace. Once I dug into the research on heart rate training, I started to limit alcohol intake, choosing better foods that would not increase my heart rate unnaturally. I added foam rolling into my training weeks and tried to keep my body healthy. I even wrote in my log, "Don't buy crap food, don't buy wine or whiskey, limit to one glass of wine when traveling." Yes, I was that serious.

Stress at home and work still weighed heavily. Traveling 70–80 percent of the time meant disrupted sleep, erratic eating, and meals on the go. Hydration often slipped through the cracks. As much as I adjusted my training to fit my lifestyle, I realized that my lifestyle itself needed a major overhaul. It's strange how once you start paying attention, you notice what triggers your heart rate to spike lack of sleep, poor nutrition, stress, travel, and, of course, my favorite, red wine.

Taking a step back to slow down brought a transformative effect I hadn't expected. As runners, many of us have this ingrained need to push through pain or rush toward the next goal. But when I actually listened to my body, healing happened in ways I hadn't anticipated. Working with a physical therapist became pivotal. Small, proactive steps like focusing on recovery and strength training made all the difference in long-term healing. At first, I didn't think I "deserved" physical therapy. It felt like something reserved for elite athletes or those who ran "fast." But when my coach suggested it, I realized I did deserve to take care of myself. Like anyone else, I needed to tend to my body, especially when pushing it to extremes. Slowing down, focusing on recovery, and staying consistent with strength training and foam rolling allowed me to run longer without pain. It was as though I had finally broken free from the self-imposed prison of discomfort.

It hit me that slowing down and prioritizing self-care turned out to be the fastest way to get back on track. As runners, we often go into denial when faced with pain, pushing ourselves to keep going instead of slowing down to take care of an injury. I had fallen into that trap, stubbornly trying to power through, convinced that stopping would only set me back. But as I took a step back, allowing myself the time to heal, I realized that this approach was actually helping me recover faster. The physical healing mirrored my mental shift. I began to understand that there was no shame in taking care of myself after all, it wasn't about getting through the race at any cost but about staying in the game for the long haul, ensuring I could finish strong rather than burning out early.

I spent the first few months of 2018 focusing on strength and heart rate, and basically relearning how to run. I had big goals for Berlin, namely, I didn't want a repeat of Chicago. I began participating in some local races and slowly rebuilt my mileage, trying my best to keep plantar fasciitis at bay. To tackle that pesky issue, I went all in with chiropractor visits, physical therapy, acupuncture, dry needling, the Graston Technique (a blade scraped across the facia; it was as horrible as it sounds), wearing a boot, custom insoles molded to my feet, and foam rolling. If it had the potential to help, I was willing to try it. I'm not sure what actually worked or if all of it contributed, but it started to slowly improve. The plantar fasciitis began to ease up in the spring of 2018, and I could now run and walk without pain.

If you've ever dealt with this type of foot pain, you know it's like that uninvited guest who lingers just a bit too long and is always there, just waiting for the perfect moment to crash the party. It never truly goes away, so I had to stay diligent with stretching and make sure I was wearing good shoes. That meant saying goodbye to many beloved stilettos and otherwise "cute" shoes in my closet that could trigger a recurrence. From then on, it was no more high heels, no more cheap footwear. Instead, I'd go with high-quality shoes with proper arch support. Sacrifices had to be made, and giving away my fun, cute shoes was definitely one of the toughest decisions I faced. Nothing says "Welcome to your fifties" like wearing sensible shoes.

Marathon training started May 30, and while I was still feeling the effects of jet lag from my Asia trip, I was excited. I had done the self-care, the strength training, the PT, and dialed in on my diet and alcohol consumption. I started making commitments to myself every week and kept them. Little achievements each week made me confident and mentally stronger on days when I wasn't feeling great.

This training program shifted the focus from mileage to "time on feet." So, instead of a traditional thirteen-mile run, I might have a two-hour run. Sometimes, there would be pace or speed work, but mostly, it was all about spending time on my feet and ensuring proper recovery, including stretching and resting like a pro napper. I'll admit I was a bit concerned about this approach. In my mind, collecting high mileage was the golden ticket to feeling prepared for 26.2 miles. It was like wearing a badge of honor that said, "Look at me, I ran X miles this week." But I also understood that recovery time was key.

Running for four hours in the heat just to hit a mileage mark could lead to a much longer recovery time before my next training run. I had to remind myself that sometimes less is more. After all, I wanted to be ready for the finish line, not just for the bragging rights of logging endless miles.

Training partners made those long, sweltering runs in July and August bearable. Berlin's timing proved brutal for those of us living in hot climates. My longest runs, scheduled for August, fell during the worst possible month, when the pavement practically sizzled like bacon. Looking back through my logs, I can see I struggled with nutrition, which led to some serious digestive issues. Let's just say my stomach often staged a protest, turning any run into a frantic dash to the nearest bathroom (at least I wasn't holding it in like that guy at the Diva race). It felt like a never-ending game of trial and error, trying to figure out what would work without turning my run into a series of emergency pit stops. What I ate leading up to long training days played a significant role. Spoiler alert: broccoli, spinach, and kale were not the best pre-run fuel. Fiber upon fiber led to many porta-john pit stops.

Before diving into the tapering phase, when I reduced my mileage during the final two weeks of training, my last twenty-mile-long run felt like a massive confidence boost.

Everything clicked. I fueled properly, kept my heart rate in check despite the heat, and managed to keep my GI system under control. It was a huge win one that reassured me I could handle the race ahead.

My friend Amanda also had a long run scheduled for the same day, so we planned to meet in the middle. We started at opposite ends of town, each of us tackling our own route. When we reached our halfway points, we high-fived each other, recharged for a moment, and then ran the remaining distance back to where we started. Having a smiling, familiar face to meet during the run made a world of difference, especially on a long training day. It turned the miles into a shared experience rather than a solitary challenge.

My coach offered a treasure trove of advice that I hadn't considered in my previous marathons. We talked about setting realistic goals, using heart rate monitors, focusing on "time on feet," and emphasizing self-care. I also learned about the "extras" that come with being a long-distance runner. Strength training, stretching, foam rolling, and perhaps the most elusive, getting enough sleep. She also told me to stop stressing about the "five-hour" thing. Let it go.

She asked me, "What are you afraid of?"

"Running another five-hour race," I told her.

"Don't focus on that. You've put in the work now execute."

Easier in theory than in practice.

Chapter 8 – Berlin Marathon 2018

"Hurricane Florence has reached Category 4 status after rapid intensification with winds over 150 mph east southeast of Cape Fear, NC. We expect landfall to be at or near Wrightsville Beach, NC, on the morning of Friday, September 14, 2018." Reported WECT News in Wilmington.

The Weather Channel was in panic mode about Hurricane Florence barreling toward Wilmington. We sat glued to the TV, watching meteorologists frantically advise everyone to prepare for evacuation, board up homes, and brace for power outages, flooding, wind damage, and flying debris. Even Jim Cantore showed up, and you know things are serious when he's in town.

Our flight was set to leave on Wednesday, September 12, right before this storm threatened to wreak havoc on our town. I kept trying to focus on the excitement of Berlin, but my mind would drift back to the impending storm. We left our dogs with my parents, crossing our fingers that our house would still be standing when we returned. A fleeting thought crossed my mind *Should I even go to Berlin? What if this massive storm hit and caused major damage to our home, our town, or our friends?*

My mom, ever the voice of reason, offered some wise words: "You can't control the storm. Staying home won't change anything. If the storm destroys your house, it'll be just as destroyed whether you're here or in Europe." Her words, though simple, grounded me in the moment. I realized she was right. Worrying wouldn't help anyone. I made the best decision I could under the circumstances and moved forward with the trip.

"It's only 'stuff,'" she said. "You can replace things." So, with that in mind, Scott and I held our breath and boarded the plane. Looking back, it's clear that this was a lot of stress to juggle, especially for someone gearing up to run a marathon.

As I mapped out my plans for Berlin, I set my A, B, and C goals. My "A" goal was to finish in under five hours because I was obsessed with a sub-five-hour race (I already wasn't listening to my coach). My "B" goal was to cross the finish line without feeling like I'd been in a five-car pileup. And my "C" goal? Well, that was simply to race without pooping at miles sixteen through eighteen.

To keep my mind focused during the race, I wrote down and memorized my mantras: "Legs are alive" and "Make yourself proud." I even considered adding "Please don't poop your pants" to the list, but I thought that might be a bit too on-the-nose.

The week before Berlin, along with the hurricane, a business trip threw a serious wrench into plans. Bad timing! This was taper time the critical phase when sleep, hydration, nutrition, and all those little race-day details mattered most. The universe seemed to conspire against me at the most crucial moment. Sleep remained elusive, meals weren't ideal, and stress crept in from every direction. Worries about the impending storm lingered. After twenty weeks of training, ready or not, it was time to go. I felt like I was prepping for a marathon on a tightrope.

We flew from Wilmington to Philadelphia on Wednesday, then on to London, and finally to Berlin, arriving the following day around dinner time. Talk about a travel marathon, it was exhausting. To combat jet lag, I chugged water like it was my new favorite sport and took some leisurely walks upon arrival, trying to convince my body to embrace local time as quickly as possible.

Even while trying to settle into our new surroundings and time zone, we were distracted by the storm back home. The news outlets were reporting that the storm was strengthening, which increased our anxiety. We watched with apprehension, unable to do anything from the other side of the world as Hurricane Florence churned into a powerful Category 4 storm and headed straight for North Carolina. We worried about our friends, family, and pets but held onto the hope that the universe would pull off a last-minute miracle and weaken the storm. We loved our beach community, and the thought of it being flattened by this monstrous storm broke our hearts. It felt surreal to be standing in the vibrant streets of Berlin, surrounded by the energy and excitement of the race, while our home and everything we cared about back in Wilmington faced such a devastating threat. The conflict between these two realities, the thrill of the marathon ahead and the fear for our home, left me feeling conflicted and helpless. I kept my fingers crossed, tried to stay focused on the task at hand, and hoped for the best outcome.

I had booked a room at the Hilton near the Konzerthaus Berlin, perfectly positioned along the marathon route. The hotel sat in the heart of a historic square, framed by magnificent buildings that dated back to 1821. Despite suffering damage during the war, the Konzerthaus continued its mission as a cultural hub, hosting music and theater performances even through the chaos of World War II, right up until its final days when bombs destroyed it. In 1977, the concert hall began to rise from the rubble when rebuilding commenced, and by 1984, the Konzerthaus reopened, restored to its former glory.

The area around the hotel exuded energy and liveliness, particularly on weekends when vibrant markets sprang up, adding to the charm of the neighborhood. With its unbeatable location, the Hilton put me just a short walk from some of Berlin's most iconic landmarks. I could easily stroll to the Brandenburg Gate the final landmark runners pass through on the marathon course and to Potsdamer Platz, the Reichstag, and other historic sites. And with the subway station right next door, exploring the city couldn't have been more convenient.

But the real cherry on top? The hotel featured a spa on the lower level, complete with a pool, multiple saunas, and massage beds. It was the perfect oasis for pre- and post-race self-care, ensuring I was pampered and ready to tackle whatever Berlin had in store.

Scott and I immersed ourselves in the history and vitality of Berlin, exploring the city's rich contrasts. Berlin had once been a tale of two cities, divided for twenty-eight years by the Berlin Wall an imposing barrier that separated communism from democracy, with Checkpoint Charlie as the symbol of that divide. Parts of the wall still stood, covered in graffiti from both sides, serving as an unmistakable testament to its tumultuous history.

It felt surreal to stand at these sites, trying to fathom what life must have been like in a place that literally kept people in and out. As I stood where the wall had once been, I couldn't help but reflect on the unimaginable sacrifices people had made, fighting, and some dying, in their desperate bids for freedom. Much of the wall had been transformed into a path of bricks, tracing the wall's former route through the city a quiet yet powerful reminder of the past.

The museums, memorials, and architecture in Berlin left a profound impact on me. Much of old Berlin had been lost to the ravages of war, but a few buildings either remained in ruins or had been carefully rebuilt to resemble their former glory. One of the most powerful experiences was visiting the Memorial to the Murdered Jews of Europe, located near the Brandenburg Gate. The memorial consists of a vast field of rectangular concrete slabs, varying in height and width, arranged in a way that suggests a wave-like movement across the landscape. The site is subtly sloped, amplifying the sensation of being engulfed as you walk through it. We could enter from any of its four sides, allowing us to immerse ourselves fully in the experience. The design aimed to replicate the disorienting and terrifying feeling Jewish families must have experienced as they saw their friends, neighbors and family one day and then lost them the next. It was a deeply emotional and haunting space, yet also an incredibly creative and thought-provoking representation.

I'd heard that many Germans, particularly Berliners, prefer not to discuss the war, yet the memorials throughout the city spoke volumes. They conveyed what words sometimes could not: the weight of history and the lessons we must never forget.

When we weren't out sightseeing, we were glued to the news about Hurricane Florence. Thankfully, just before making landfall in Wrightsville Beach, the storm weakened and was downgraded to a Category 1. My parents had evacuated to East Tennessee, enduring hours of bumper-to-bumper traffic with our two poodles, who probably thought they were on the world's least glamorous road trip. When they made it back, the universe seemed to throw one last obstacle their way. They hit even worse traffic than before, a cruel reminder that nothing ever goes as planned. We were just grateful they eventually returned home safely.

Even though the intensity of the storm had decreased before landfall, the aftermath of Hurricane Florence hit Wilmington hard. Flooding turned the town into a waterlogged mess, and with Interstate 40 closed, getting supplies in and out became a game of Tetris strategizing, shifting, and hoping things would fall into place. Watching our friends struggle online, some without power, some wading through knee-deep water to get essentials, served as a harsh reminder that no matter how prepared we think we are, nature has its own plans.

While we were preoccupied with worrying about home, we also managed to do an absurd amount of walking. And when I say "absurd," I mean we walked way too much. Looking back, it was a massive rookie mistake. The day before the race, we made a wrong turn getting off the subway and ended up walking for four miles in *flip-flops*. Yes, flip-flops. At the time, I thought I was just taking in the sights, but by the end of the day, my feet were filing a formal complaint.

How could I resist? Berlin was a mesmerizing city, full of history and charm at every turn. I felt like a kid in a candy store, and honestly, my eyes were bigger than my legs could handle. The Berlin TV Tower, rotating gracefully high above the city, stood as a must-see landmark, especially at sunset. I met up with some friends who were also running the race, and we gathered for food and drinks. Between bites and sips, we snapped selfies and took in the stunning views, letting the golden light of sunset paint the city in a magical glow.

As we explored more, I couldn't help but marvel at the stark contrast between East and West Berlin. It was like walking through two different time periods. The East side, with its post-war rapid construction, exuded a more utilitarian vibe as if they were just trying to rebuild and get by. Meanwhile, West Berlin oh, West Berlin seemed to be saying, "Let's impress the tourists!" The architecture had a flair, like a city trying to outdo itself, striving for beauty and charm, the kind of city that said, "You'll never forget me."

The night before the race, we went to a restaurant where I ate the blandest meal imaginable chicken, potatoes, and a few green beans. That was it. No pasta, no rice, no hearty carbs to fuel me up. In other words, I didn't carb-load at all. To make matters worse, I didn't hydrate properly after all the walking we had done around the city. I should've been drinking water and electrolytes all day and, ideally, carb-loading for the previous three days. Race day was shaping up to be warm and sunny, and I knew the importance of sitting with my feet up, relaxing, and mentally preparing, but instead, I had been rushing through sightseeing, burning energy I couldn't afford to lose.

Even though I had trained in the heat all summer, running a marathon in full sun and warm temperatures was an entirely different beast. Heat on race day adds a level of exhaustion that no training could truly replicate. My body could handle the summer runs, but this? This was going to be a test. A big one.

Race morning arrived warm, sunny, and with perfect blue skies, basically a runner's nightmare. I met up with my friend Mailyn, who had survived the Chicago marathon alongside me. Armed with a bottle of water and a banana (the breakfast of runners), we made our way to the starting area. Scott decided to play the role of finish line cheerleader this time since he had a hard time locating me in London, and his talent for finding me in a crowd was a work in progress.

As we chatted in the corral, we found ourselves in a long line for the porta-johns a classic marathon experience. It gave us a chance to connect with a woman from New York who was worried about being swept off the course. She considered herself a slower runner, and I could tell she wasn't sure if she could go the distance. We reassured her, and in doing so, we reassured ourselves, too. We reminded each other that today wasn't just about finishing but soaking in the energy and excitement of being part of a World Marathon Major.

The Berlin Marathon kicked off near the Victory Column, an iconic landmark commemorating a war victory from the 1860s. The column stood proudly in the Tiergarten, a sprawling park in the center of Berlin. It's positioned on a roundabout, so runners get to choose which side of the circle they run around. From above, it looked stunning, a perfect visual representation of the race's grandeur. What made this race inspiring was knowing that world marathon record holder Eliud Kipchoge was running ahead of us. Although way ahead of us, the thought that we were running the same route felt exciting. His legend loomed over us, and it gave me an extra boost, even though I knew we were in two entirely different races he was shooting for another world record, and I was simply about crossing the finish line. But still, to share that course with someone like him felt magical.

After several more trips to the porta-johns, we finally lined up, and the crowd began a slow clap. Clap, pause, clap, pause. Gradually, it picked up speed, turning into a thunderous cheer that sent chills down my spine. The energy at the start of the marathon was nothing short of electric, contagious, and enough to make you forget all about those pre-race jitters.

The German national anthem was played, the gun went off, and we were crossing the start line timing mat, officially running the Berlin Marathon. The sun beat down, but I tried not to stress about it. I'd trained in the sweltering heat all summer, putting in the miles through brutal conditions.

But as we began, I immediately struggled with the heat. The sun felt intense, more so than I'd expected. Even so, I tried to stay focused on my pace and the rhythm of the race, trying to keep my mind clear. The excitement of being here, running through the streets of Berlin, pushed me forward. We ran past the beautiful Victory Column, and I kicked off my trusty run/walk method. We passed by Moabit Prison and the Bundeskanzleramt, the German Chancellor's seat, before reaching Rosenthaler Platz near the ten-mile mark. It was a beautiful stretch, but as I cruised through this area, I felt my body start to change and a warning siren going off in my brain.

Suddenly, a sharp, intense cramping gripped my shoulders, so severe it felt like I was running with a pair of twenty-five-pound weights strapped to my back. I hadn't even reached a third of the way and already the dreaded "wall" loomed large on the horizon. Talk about an uninvited guest crashing the party. The pain made every step feel like a monumental effort, and just when I thought it couldn't get worse, my mind began to spiral, feeding into the discomfort. I had hit "the wall," a dreaded place where runners never want to enter. When the wall hits, it feels like your body has flipped a switch and says, "Nope, you're not running another step."

Never had I experienced such a struggle so early in a race just ten miles in, so naturally, I started to panic. *What was happening? Why couldn't I run like I was supposed to?* In a moment of frustration, I texted Scott, hoping for some comforting words, maybe a little boost of encouragement. But when I looked down at my phone, his reply hit like a cold slap to the face: 5:20 expected finish time. *WHAT!?*

Now, I found myself in full-on freak-out mode. The thought of finishing worse than I had in Chicago seemed unbearable. My "A" goal the one I had worked so hard for slipped through my fingers, and the harsh truth hit me like a ton of bricks: I faced five hours in the heat, in pain, and feeling miserable. This marathon, the one I had hoped would be my redemption, morphed into a nightmare. And the worst part? The fear that this was only the beginning. Gnawing at me with every painful step was the thought that things might not improve, that I might never recover from this mental and physical collapse. I couldn't shake the feeling that the race wasn't just hard it felt like it was breaking me.

I limped along, mostly walking but running when I could. I passed through more "platzes" or plaza areas. Suddenly, nature called, and I found myself in dire need of a porta-john, but none were in sight. By the time I hit mile sixteen, I was desperate and nearly in tears thinking I was going to poop my pants and have to run the rest of the race just like that guy at the Diva Half Marathon. My punishment for making fun of him. Finally, like a mirage, I spotted a construction site with a porta-john.

I stumbled upon the most disgusting yet strangely beautiful portable toilet I'd ever seen. It looked like it hadn't been emptied in months. Covering my mouth and nose, I fought the urge to gag. It was a biohazard, but at that moment, I didn't care. More late-race GI distress frustrated me, and my "C" goal racing without pooping was officially out the window. All that was left was my "B" goal: finish.

With no other choice, I leaned on sheer willpower, stubbornness, and a whole lot of prayer to make it to the finish line. Every step was a struggle, but there was no turning back. I'd come too far to let this race defeat me.

While it was a pleasant seventy-five degrees for the spectators, for us marathoners, it felt like we were running on the surface of the sun. I kept daydreaming about Scott waiting for me at the finish line, the promised free beer from the race organizers, and the glorious Epsom salt bath that would follow. Honestly, anything to distract myself from this horrific slog of a marathon. Mile after mile, I dreamed of washing my hair, lying down on the ground, and being anywhere but there.

Berlin had water stations that were a runner's oasis, complete with water fountains that were a divine gift from the hydration gods. The water was cold and refreshing. As the heat took its toll, they started bringing out misters and cooling towels like they were giving us spa treatments mid-race.

I found myself running ten steps, walking ten steps, and repeating this awkward dance like I was stuck at the most uncomfortable party. It was all my body could manage. Disappointment and confusion washed over me. It felt like my body and mind were locked in a heated debate, with my brain calling all the shots. The worst part? I had no choice but to follow its lead. After hour upon hour of this torture, the Brandenburg Gate came into view, a glorious site built in 1791 and stood as a symbol of unity and division alike. It was one of the most beautiful architectural sites in the world, and that day, it was the most beautiful thing I'd ever seen. Everyone had warned me that the finish line wasn't at the gate itself. I must run through it and then tackle a few more tenths to the actual finish.

Seeing that gate gave me a surge of determination, and though I likely shuffled, I picked up my pace. Quitting never crossed my mind not even for a second. I would have crawled if it came to that. With a final burst of whatever energy I had left, I raised my arms in triumph and crossed the finish line in 5:22:35.

I did it. I finished. Devastated, confused, sad, yet oddly happy. The walk from the finish line to the family area felt like navigating a never-ending, twisted maze leading to the ultimate reward: an Erlanger beer. As I shuffled along, sipping my beer, tears mixed with smiles, my emotions collided in a wild swirl. I had just completed my third World Major. It wasn't pretty, nor was it what I'd imagined, but there was no doubt I earned that medal. And by God, I was wearing it for a week straight.

Scott, ever supportive, never once mentioned my finish time. All he said was, "You finished. Nothing else matters." In that moment, I realized he was right. I had survived the most miserable slog of my life, pushed through every obstacle, and crossed the finish line with a medal in hand. That was all that truly mattered.

The finish area unfolded against the stunning backdrop of the Reichstag, a magnificent government building dating back to the late 1800s. Scott and I had toured it just the day before, and I couldn't resist snapping a thousand photos. The architecture inside had taken my breath away. While we were running, Mailyn's husband, Todd, an artist, had seized the opportunity to paint this historic landmark. His finished piece was nothing short of spectacular. A reminder that not everything was about running.

To my relief, Scott had arranged for a rickshaw ride back to our hotel, sparing me the agony of shuffling along like a zombie. As we rolled through the streets, I spotted the woman from New York the one we had chatted with at the porta-john that morning. The sweeper was right on her tail, and I felt a rush of empathy. This was not the ending anyone had hoped for. I jumped out of the rickshaw like a superhero, wobbling my way over to her.

"You got this girl! You can do this! Just a little bit more! I believe in you!" I shouted to her. I gave her as much encouragement as I could muster. I'm not sure if she remembered me, but I hoped my little pep talk helped her keep moving. Nothing says "I care" quite like a stranger sprinting (well, more like stumbling) to cheer you at the end of a marathon.

After a wonderful soaking, refueling, and resting, I met up with some friends from Switzerland who had also run the race. We shared an amazing meal, relived the day, and laughed at all the crazy things we'd seen and experienced. As we reminisced, I couldn't shake the confusion and sadness about my performance. In the months following the race, it hit me like a ton of bricks: I had walked way too much before the race and didn't fuel or carb-load properly. Add in the stress of work, and the havoc of a hurricane hitting our hometown, and I realized I'd started the race already depleted.

Oh, and let's not forget that this training cycle was twenty weeks long, which was a bit ambitious compared to my usual sixteen-week plan. Sure, I felt good until I realized I had probably peaked two weeks before the race during that fun twenty-mile training run where I high-fived Amanda and felt everything click.

My coach said to me, "Marathons are hard, yo." Nothing could be truer. They're like that tough-love friend who teaches you something about yourself every time, only if you're willing to learn. I was absorbing all the lessons like a sponge and determined to come back stronger. After scribbling down notes post-race to capture my feelings, I got real. Let's face it: there's a tiny percentage of people in the world who run marathons, especially women over fifty. I was doing epic things. How many people can say they've traversed 26.2 miles? In reality, no one cared about my finish time except me. I spent so much energy stressing about not going over five hours that I inadvertently manifested it.

I heard author, podcaster, and former monk Jay Shetty call it "the rule of the most repeated thought." Jay said, "You will manifest your most repeated thought." Boy, I did, in spades. What I thought, said, and believed became my reality.

Many coaches and runners will tell you to "run the mile you're in." Wise words, indeed. In Berlin, I learned that just because I felt like I was dragging a boulder behind me at mile ten didn't mean things couldn't turn around. If I had focused more on hydrating and enjoying the experience instead of fixating on a finish time, I might've run better and actually had fun.

Eliud Kipchoge went on to set a new world marathon record that day, finishing in an astonishing 2:01:39 about 4:30 per mile for the full marathon. One of his signature statements, "No human is limited," resonates with runners everywhere. He even went on to run a non-sanctioned sub-two-hour marathon in Vienna, earning him the title of the greatest marathoner of all time. Sharing the same marathon course where he set that world record was thrilling. These achievements created a giddy vibe in the city and left us amateurs in awe.

Scott and I left Berlin the following day and flew to Munich to extend our trip, where the airport greeted us with complete madness. Thankfully, we had given ourselves plenty of time to navigate through security. I humbly wore my medal and jacket, proud of my accomplishment. Sure, my marathon time didn't set any records, but I finished. And that medal? It became my badge of honor, one I planned to wear all week.

Scott had regained much of his strength and health, allowing us to enjoy the trip. But a quiet storm was brewing beneath the surface. It started with a nagging tooth pain that seemed innocuous at first. He brushed it off, thinking it was just a cavity or an old filling needing attention. What we didn't realize was that this was the calm before the storm the start of a new battle, one far more intense than the cancer fight we thought we had left behind. Looking back, I often say, "Cancer was a breeze compared to what came after." The road ahead would test us in ways we never imagined. I realized nothing could have prepared us for the challenges, the stress, and the heartbreak that would follow. It felt like the universe had thrown us back into the fire, but this time, the flames were different. This time, it wasn't just about survival.

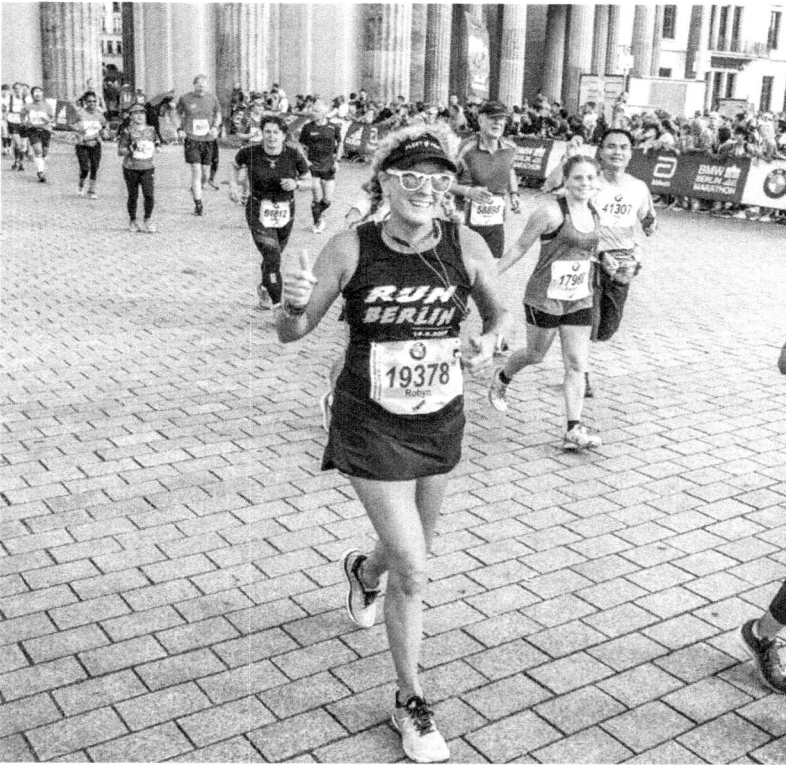

Berlin Marathon, September 16, 2018

Chapter 9 – Time to Get Real

As we flew back into Wilmington, the scale of destruction left by Hurricane Florence became painfully clear. From the sky, the flooded streets and submerged homes stood as a stark reminder of nature's unforgiving power. The vast swaths of water, the downed trees, and the disorder below painted a picture of devastation. It was humbling to witness, and as we descended, I felt an overwhelming sense of helplessness mixed with the relief of being home, knowing that the real work was just beginning.

We were fortunate to find that neither our home nor my parents' home had sustained any damage. Reuniting with our poodles was a joyous moment; they were ecstatic to be back in their familiar surroundings. Almost immediately, I jumped into action, volunteering with the Cajun Navy to help organize supplies for families in need. My employer graciously gave me time off to volunteer, allowing me to focus on making a difference in our community during this challenging time. It felt good to leave running alone for a few weeks and focus on other priorities.

Before Berlin, Scott had started experiencing troubling tooth pain. He went to the dentist, and after a root canal, we thought we had put the issue to rest. Unbeknownst to us, lurking beneath his teeth and gums was a much larger problem. The effects of radiation had caused significant damage to his gums, teeth, and jawbone, primarily cutting off blood flow. When blood flow diminishes, tissues begin to die. And when the body detects this decay, it goes into survival mode, trying to expel what it sees as a threat. What we thought was a simple dental issue was, in reality, the beginning of a long and miserable journey filled with unexpected challenges.

Scott developed a hole in his gum, and a portion of his jawbone became exposed and started to push out. Eating became problematic (again), and the pain increased day by day. Scott's radiation oncologist and his ENT doctors both recommended a maxillofacial surgeon here in Wilmington who specialized in orthoradial necrosis (ORN) and jaw reconstructive surgeries. He suggested a small surgery where he would clean out the dead bone, extract bone marrow from Scott's hip, layer and pack it in the gum, and hope it would close up and heal. After the surgery, he told me that this only works about 25 percent of the time. He was right. Scott experienced the other 75 percent first- hand.

Running marathons took a backseat as we focused on navigating Scott's jaw issues and, once again, the slow deterioration of his health. The jaw pain combined with his limited swallowing capabilities made eating extremely difficult, and he started to lose weight steadily. The thrill of running and traveling was replaced by doctor visits and consultations as we grappled with the reality of his condition. It was a difficult adjustment, but we remained determined to face this challenge together, searching for hope amid the struggles.

Scott decided to explore hyperbaric chamber therapy, believing it might offer the relief he desperately sought. For six weeks, he spent two hours every day in a pressurized tube, hoping it would boost blood flow to the affected areas and aid in healing. Though the sessions were relaxing, he noticed no real improvement, and his frustration mounted.

Determined not to give up, Scott turned to pain management. He underwent two pain blocks and a nerve ablation, even trying Botox injections in a bid to alleviate his suffering. Yet, with each new treatment, disappointment followed; none of these therapies provided the relief he desperately needed. As the pain persisted, Scott felt increasingly trapped in a cycle of hope and despair, searching for a solution that remained just out of reach.

We watched helplessly as more bone became exposed, the pain intensifying with each passing day. To complicate the issue further, while his jawbone deteriorated, an infection took root deep within. This infection manifested as a painful lump on the side of his face, freaking us out as it looked like another tumor.

Despite being prescribed Oxycodone for the pain, relief remained elusive. The situation took a dark turn as Scott began a troubling routine of coming home from work, popping an Oxy, and washing it down with two beers. The combination blurred the lines between coping and fear, leaving him in a dark place. With Scott's health rapidly declining and his spirits following suit, a crushing sense of urgency settled over us. He felt the weighted hand of desperation tightening around his chest, and it became painfully clear that he couldn't continue down this path much longer. It was time to stop hoping for things to get better on their own and search for a definitive answer. We both knew that if we didn't act now, the battle would slip further out of his reach.

In a bid to relieve his suffering, the surgeon performed another small surgery to remove more dead bone and attempt to close the gum again. The prognosis was not good: Scott's jaw was extremely fragile, and he would be restricted to soft foods for six weeks.

After the procedure, the surgeon pulled me aside, his expression grave.

"We need to get real," he said. "I can't keep doing these cleanup surgeries. There is very little bone left, and his jaw is going to break into pieces." He went on to explain that the next step involved jaw reconstruction.

We had decisions to make, and they were not easy decisions. The jaw reconstruction surgery was massive and involved a lot of other body parts. The surgeon would remove Scott's existing teeth, jaw, and gum, and replace them with a six-inch piece of his fibula (leg bone). The surgery would last over ten hours and would require at least two nights in intensive care plus an additional seven to ten days in a step-down unit. At one point, we were able to meet another patient who had gone through this same surgery and had recovered and was living a mostly normal life.

We discussed at length his options, which weren't many.

On November 12, 2018, Scott underwent a twelve-hour Mandibulectomy and Fibula Free Flap Reconstruction at New Hanover Regional Medical Center with two surgeons working in tandem. On that crucial day, Scott's sister Alison was by my side in the hospital, providing much-needed support. My parents took care of our dogs, ensuring they were loved and safe. Even my friend Nicole dropped by the hospital to offer a comforting hug and words of encouragement. It was a long day, but the presence of loved ones helped carry me through.

Once the surgeon removed the six-inch piece of bone and skin from Scott's leg, the other surgeon meticulously opened his jaw. They replaced his jawbone with the leg bone, using a titanium "chain" to hold it together, and used screws to install dental implants. The day stretched on, tense and filled with uncertainty. Alison and I walked the hospital corridors, trying to keep our minds occupied. We talked, played cornhole in the hospital courtyard, ate several times in the cafeteria, walked, and talked some more.

At last, the surgeon paged me. My heart raced as I sat down with him to get an update. The surgery was over, he said, and had been successful, but I struggled to process his words. My mind was a whirlwind, and I don't remember a lot of what he said.

Standing outside the ICU, surrounded by others anxiously awaiting to see their loved ones, I couldn't help but notice the gravity of the life-threatening situations all around us. The sight of these distressed spouses, children, and parents weighed heavily on me, making it difficult to hold back my own tears before I even saw Scott.

When we were allowed into the ICU, the floodgates opened. Both Alison and I began to cry at the sight of him. He lay there, unconscious and almost unrecognizable, a web of wires and tubes enveloping him. His throat was stitched from ear to chin. My heart ached, a mix of fear and sorrow swelling within me. But as I glanced at his amazing nurse diligently caring for him, a flicker of reassurance cut through my despair. In that moment, I knew he was in good hands, but the road ahead seemed endless.

Scott spent a couple of days in the ICU, closely monitored for vascular activity. The looming threat of a blood clot hung over him. If one formed, the doctors would have to tear everything out and start from scratch. Eventually, he was transferred to a step-down unit, which became our home away from home for the next eight days.

In this new space, Scott faced numerous challenges. A feeding tube snaked through his nose; a wound vac clung to his leg to help close and heal the incision that went from his knee to his ankle; and a significant skin graft on his upper thigh used to close the incisions made to his jawline. Additionally, he'd had a tracheostomy to provide an airway. He coughed incessantly as nurses, technicians, and therapists flowed in and out of the room like a never-ending tide.

Scott was restless and irritable. He constantly felt hot and desperately wanted a fan to blow cool air on him. Pain and discomfort were his unwelcome companions, and he struggled to find any semblance of contentment, whether lying down or sitting up. With speaking nearly impossible, he resorted to scribbling on a notepad to communicate how he felt and what he needed. Each note was a glimpse into his frustration trying to navigate this experience.

I was juggling daily trips to the hospital with little time for running, but I had planned to join a group run for an early morning escape, hoping to squeeze in a few miles to relieve the mountain of stress weighing on me. Just as I was getting dressed, my phone buzzed with a frantic text from Scott.

"Can you come to the hospital now? I'm having an emergency."

Confused, I texted back. "Did you call the nurse?"

"I've been calling, but no one will come. Please, come now, I'm bleeding."

His message sent a chill down my spine. *He said he had been calling for a nurse, but no one would come to his room*, I thought. My heart raced as dread settled in. I dropped everything and drove as fast as I could to the hospital, my heart pounding with each passing second. In my panic, I sprinted from the parking lot all the way to the front doors, charging through and slapping the up-button for the elevator over and over, desperate to reach him.

What I found in his room stopped me in my tracks: blood spraying in an arc across the room from his trachea, and the terror in Scott's eyes was unmistakable. Time seemed to freeze as I took in the scene, the gravity of the moment crashing over me. I felt a surge of adrenaline mixed with sheer panic, knowing I had to act quickly. I started yelling, then screaming for help. The hallway and nurses' station were deserted. I screamed louder, found an alarm on the wall, and hit it over and over, my heart racing as hysteria washed over me, tears streaming down my face.

Moments later, crash carts began to arrive, and suddenly, the room filled with nurses and medical staff, their presence a flurry of action and urgency. Thankfully, our surgeon's physician assistant was already on his way into the hospital when the alarm sounded, and he reached Scott's bedside within minutes. It turned out that the trachea tube had nicked a vein during one of Scott's coughing spells. Fortunately, it wasn't life-threatening. Relief washed over me, mingling with the adrenaline of those harrowing moments.

Once we got him cleaned up and somewhat comfortable again, I sat on his bed and broke down, sobbing uncontrollably. I had truly thought he was dying. He patted my back, offering quiet comfort as I let my emotions spill over. I cried all day, unable to stop, no matter how hard I tried. My tears flowed as I spoke to nurses, doctors, PAs, respiratory therapists, and various other hospital staff. It was the worst day of my life.

Scott began working with a physical therapist right away, determined to start walking again. Each day, he made strides, moving through the hospital halls and showing remarkable improvement. However, with multiple wounds to manage, keeping him stocked with medications, addressing his care, and ensuring he ate became a full-time job for all of us.

We were utterly exhausted, navigating the emotional rollercoaster together. We cried when I accidentally smashed his finger in the door. We laughed when I tried to use dry shampoo on his hair because he hadn't showered in ten days.

We felt a huge wave of relief when it was time to go home. Armed with a ridiculously long list of instructions, I hoped I could tackle Scott's recovery by cleaning and rebandaging his wounds, and setting up a medication and feeding schedule, all while trying to keep my job and manage the dogs, who were looking for ways to snuggle on his lap.

Scott, bless him, was grumpy, in pain, and frustrated, which made him a delightful patient. Managing his medications felt like a part-time job. He was practically downing gallons of Oxycodone, and each trip to the pharmacy became a test of my patience. I had a few moments of, let's face it, complete meltdowns in CVS parking lots when they looked at me like I was trying to score drugs. I drove all over town trying to get his pain medicines filled. No single pharmacy had enough liquid Oxy to keep up with his dosage schedule.

To say I had a lot on my plate would be the understatement of the century. I kept running whenever I could and spent the time I had doing yoga to stay grounded. I was still working full-time, and once Scott came home from the hospital, I took on the role of his nurse.

After an overwhelming first week of working with the home health nurse, fumbling through wound care and medication administration, we finally settled into a routine. Things began to feel more manageable. Scott wore a boot for three months, and while the surgeon estimated an eight-week recovery for his jaw, it turned out to be more like two years. The journey was grueling, filled with infections, endless gallons of liquid Oxy, numerous complications, and countless hours of pain and frustration. Our surgeon repeatedly reminded us that each complication occurred in only about 10 percent of cases. Guess who was squarely in that 10 percent? Scott seemed to collect complications like lucky charms.

Through all this chaos, running became my saving grace. Even while neck-deep in one of the most stressful times of my life, I felt ready to set a new goal. My friend Pam, who I had run the London Marathon with, sent me a note saying there were charities offering entries for the 2020 Boston Marathon. She encouraged me to apply.

Entering the Boston Marathon was no easy feat, especially since runners must qualify based on their marathon times. For someone like me, who ran on the slower side, it felt nearly impossible. Many runners share this predicament and turn to charity running, making the charity route increasingly competitive. I realized that as charity entries became more popular, the fundraising minimums would likely climb higher. So, I figured it was time to take a shot at it.

I braced myself for the reality of the charity minimums, typically hovering around $8,500, with some even reaching $10,000. *Was I out of my mind to think I could raise that much money while managing a very sick husband, working a full-time job, and training for another marathon?* Yes, probably, but I quickly learned that Boston-charity running was notoriously competitive, and I figured if I didn't go for it now, fundraising amounts would be out of reach in the future. We had to interview with charities and convince them we were the right runner for their team. They hit us with lengthy questionnaires about fundraising strategies, experience, and reasons for wanting to partner with their cause. Then came the phone interview, which felt more like a job interview. We had to convince the organizers we were the right runner for their charity team.

To be honest, it all felt a bit disingenuous. We all knew the main reason for applying to run for charity was an entry into the Boston Marathon. I kept those thoughts to myself, told them what they wanted to hear, and thankfully, I was chosen. Once I was in, my sales background kicked in, and I started planning and setting milestones to reach my fundraising goal. The key to success was to create a plan that could be broken down into manageable steps and then execute those tasks.

In the Fall of 2019, my goals were to raise $8,500 for a Boston charity, run the Boston Marathon in April 2020, and exceed my work quota and win a free trip to Greece, all while helping Scott get back to a healthy status. I'd always heard that if you want something done, give it to a busy person. I certainly qualified. Armed with goals and milestones, all I had to do was get busy and execute.

I marked important dates on my calendar for fundraising and planned events to help collect larger amounts of cash at once. My goal was to raise at least $5,000 by December 31, 2019. I figured if I could hit my end-of-year goal, I'd be more than halfway there and could take it a bit easier until the April 2020 deadline. I'd seen many comments online about how runners often feel uncomfortable asking friends and family for money. While it can be tough, people genuinely wanted to help, especially if I shared my story and opened up about my journey. The first rule of fundraising was simple: don't be afraid to ask for money. I started with crowdfunding on Facebook, LinkedIn, Instagram, and through emails. To my surprise, the donations came flooding in quickly.

I organized a couple of fundraisers with local restaurants and they donated a portion of the food sales to my charity. I ended up making close to $800, but it was a lot of work standing out in the cold, handing out flyers, and asking folks to show them when ordering. Thankfully, my running club rallied around me and helped drive up sales, combining it with a group run for added fun.

Next, I reached out to a local race director and arranged to be paid twenty-five dollars for each volunteer I signed up to help with a half marathon in Wilmington. Once again, my running club, along with some non-running friends, stepped up to volunteer their time. After recruiting twenty people, I quickly raised another $500, and I could feel my fundraising efforts gaining momentum. I steadily made progress toward my goal and little by little, the contributions added up plus, I was enjoying the process of raising money.

While managing the fundraising efforts, interviews with local coaches began. Seeking a personal touch, my goal was to find someone who could run with me, assess my gait, and offer hands-on advice. I chose seasoned Boston Marathoner and former collegiate runner Coach Rhonda. Rhonda had done her homework. She knew about my Six Star Medal goal and was familiar with my marathon history. After sharing my aim for a personal best in Boston, I felt a renewed sense of determination. With no lingering injuries to hold me back and the benefits of cool months of winter training, the time felt right to set a big goal one that would push me beyond my limits. I also started working with Diana, a local nutritionist, and she was an absolute game-changer for me. I've since told her countless times how much she's helped me, and it only took one or two appointments to work wonders on my diet. She took a look at what I was eating and drinking, and with a few tweaks, I was able to make great strides in managing my gut issues. The biggest change we made was limiting fiber leading up to race day. I had been chowing down on too many veggies before long runs, which made for some rather unpleasant trips to the porta-john. After avoiding veggies my entire life, I'd done a complete 180 and learned to love them, so giving them up before races felt like a betrayal. But soon enough, I realized it was essential.

Then came multi-day carb-loading, which I had never attempted before. I focused on getting "good carbs" like quinoa, rice, and whole grains into my body, but also "fun carbs" like pretzels, potatoes, and Kit Kats (my weakness). I also loaded up on electrolytes, water, and Gatorade. Carb-loading wasn't exactly a walk in the park. The first time I tried it, I felt like a balloon. Ridiculously bloated.

There were online calculators to help me figure out how many carbs I needed based on my weight and other factors, but trust me, the math got overwhelming. I ended up creating a spreadsheet detailing the foods I needed to eat and their carb count. I gradually increased my intake leading up to the day before a long training run, when I aimed for the biggest carb fest. Again, not the most comfortable experience. Imagine walking around with a big, bloated gut. But I found that for me, it was essential, and it made a significant difference in my running.

Like I had planned, I hit my $5,000 fundraising goal by the end of the year. On top of that, my work team crushed our sales quota, and we won the trip to Greece. It was shaping up to be an epic year. Here I was set to run the Boston Marathon and, a month later, jet off to Greece with my work team and our families. I was ready for 2020 to be the best year ever. Yes, 2020, best year ever! Then the universe said, "Not so fast."

My training was going phenomenally. I was having the best cycle of my life. With no injuries and my diet dialed in, I was nailing faster splits during my tempo runs and tackling hills like a pro. I even traveled to Raleigh to run hills in Umstead State Park with some amazing friends who showed up to support me. I alternated my run/walk ratio between a four-minute run followed by a thirty-second walk and then a two-minute run with a thirty-second walk. My coach wasn't familiar with the run/walk method, so we tweaked it for my long runs. I'd start running for a couple of miles, switch to the run/walk, and then finish strong by running the last mile or two with no walk breaks. Rhonda's famous "last mile, best mile" mantra in my head.

At the end of February 2020, Coach Rhonda, my high-fiving friend Amanda, and local Wilmington running legend, Brenda headed to Atlanta to spectate at the 2020 Marathon Olympic Trials. It was a fantastic opportunity to see world-class American marathoners in action, and we had three local women who had qualified to compete. After the trials, there was a half marathon for the "rest of us" on Sunday, which was a perfect tune-up for Boston, right at the halfway point in our training. While we each had different goals, we were all excited to run the streets of Atlanta.

Race day for the Olympic Trials was blustery and cold. The runners competed on a loop course, allowing us to see them multiple times throughout the race. Watching athletes like Des Linden, Emily Sisson, Aliphine Tuliamuk, and newcomer Molly Seidel was incredibly inspiring. We dashed around the course, getting chills at the finish area as these women poured their hearts into securing their Olympic spots. Their speed, form, grit, and determination were impressive.

The next day, the weather was perfect for running our half marathon. It was cool with no wind. I chose to maintain a steady marathon pace rather than "race" it. I wasn't aiming for a personal best or an age group award. I stuck to my plan, even though I felt a bit of FOMO watching my friends push themselves. In the end, I finished in 2:12 at a 10:03-minute pace with a negative split. Mission accomplished! The event was a blast, and we capped off the weekend with shopping, tequila, and sushi. We were all on top of the world. What could go wrong?

The next day, March 1, 2020, the world flipped upside down. The pandemic hit the United States right when we arrived at the Atlanta airport slightly hungover and bleary-eyed, surrounded by a crowd of runners, their families, and fans all leaving town. I remember clearing my throat as I walked through the metal detector, and a TSA employee yelled at me to put on a mask. Mask? What mask? I'd never worn a mask. Up until that day, COVID-19 felt like a distant rumor, like that one friend who always says they'll show up but never does.

At the time, we thought it would be just a couple of weeks before we could resume our normal lives. But nope, not even close. Events started canceling left and right, and while Boston was still a month and a half away, we were all naively optimistic. *COVID would be gone, right? We'd be able to gather thirty-five thousand runners, right? And my Greece trip in May? Absolutely no way that would get canceled.*

Day by day, reality set in. I had met my fundraising goal, crushed my training workouts, and was ready for an epic marathon. Then came the news: the Boston Athletic Association (BAA) canceled the race. Soon after, my company pulled the plug on our trip to Greece. Everything went virtual like a bad Zoom meeting that no one wanted to attend. It was heartbreaking, gut-wrenching, and all sorts of frustrating.

To make matters worse, Scott was fighting off persistent infections in his "new" jaw, each day a battle of high-dose antibiotics, feverish nights, and the struggle to eat. We were trapped in a never-ending nightmare. My own strength began to crack under the weight of it all. One afternoon, the pressure finally crushed me. I sank to my knees in the living room, the load too much to bear. The tears came first, pouring down in torrents, followed by sobs so raw, so violent, they felt like they might tear me apart. It was as if every ounce of grief, fear, and frustration I had been holding in for months exploded all at once, and I couldn't stop it. I couldn't breathe through it. I couldn't escape it. In that moment, I felt as if the world was closing in on me, as though the universe itself had conspired to deliver every possible blow all at once. It wasn't just the illness, the uncertainty, or the pain. It was the suffocating weight of hopelessness that I couldn't outrun. All I wanted was a sliver of relief, a glimmer of light in the darkness, but the fear and helplessness had me trapped. I felt utterly lost, swallowed by the overwhelming tide of despair.

I cried so hard my abdominal muscles ached for days afterward. The kind of deep, soul-shattering sobs that left me gasping for air, as if I could shed the weight of all the grief, all the frustration, in those moments. But then came the anger. I was furious. Furious that my husband, the person who had been my rock, had to endure cancer as well as the aftereffects. Furious about the pain, the heartbreak, the devastation that had obliterated our lives. I mourned the smallest, simplest things. We had lost the lunch outings we used to look forward to, now impossible because Scott couldn't eat or swallow. How could something as basic as eating together be taken away? And then, the anger grew darker, more personal. I had poured my heart into training for the Boston Marathon and begged friends, coworkers, and family for donations, for their support, to make this dream a reality. It had consumed me, but now it slipped away like sand through my fingers. The marathon, the chance to be a part of something bigger than myself, disappeared.

I had crushed my work goals, and pushed myself harder than I ever thought possible in my career. And now? Now, there would be no reward, no trip of a lifetime with my team, no chance to experience the magic of Greece with the people I had worked so hard to get there with. Everything felt like it had been ripped away, and I couldn't shake the sense of injustice. I had given everything, and the universe had nothing to offer in return but silence. On top of all of that pain, I wrestled with a crushing guilt for feeling angry when I was healthy. *How could I complain?* People were sick and dying by the thousands. *Who was I to be upset about a marathon or a trip to Greece? These were first-world problems, right?* Yet, the anger was still there, boiling beneath the surface. I woke up in the middle of the night fuming, so mad that I couldn't go back to sleep and would stew until dawn.

The carefully constructed house of cards I'd built convincing myself I could handle anything collapsed around me. I felt trapped in a fury of emotions, unable to escape. For the first time, I recognized I needed help. I couldn't outrun this turmoil. Running had once been my refuge, but now it felt like a poor substitute for the raging storm within.

One of my high school friends, a breast cancer survivor, once told me I needed to be a rock for Scott. She advised that if I needed to cry, scream, or throw a tantrum, I should do it with my friends and not let him see me lose my composure. It was sound advice; it helped Scott navigate those tough days and nights, but it was incredibly challenging for me. What we were going through felt like a heavy weight on my chest, and I didn't want to burden my family or friends. I felt so alone in my sadness. I knew I needed help, but it took me months to muster the courage to make an appointment with a therapist.

Like many people, I thought I could handle everything on my own and didn't need anyone to listen to my problems. Plus, with Scott facing so much, I felt he was the one who deserved the help. I was healthy, so what right did I have to complain? Yet, sleepless nights and the weight of the pandemic made it clear I was struggling to cope. Fortunately, I had friends who helped me realize that I deserved support, too, even if my struggles weren't physical. I needed to take care of myself to be strong for Scott and for my own life. But full disclosure: calling a therapist was the hardest thing I've ever had to do. I don't know why seeking mental health help was so hard, but making that call turned out to be the best decision of my life.

At first, talking about my issues felt surprisingly difficult. I'm usually an open book with my friends, so why was it so tough with a therapist? Sure, she was a stranger, but I'm a talker. By our second session, I confidently declared that I was "cured" and didn't need therapy anymore. I convinced myself that talking about my problems wouldn't yield any results. What I didn't want to admit was the depth of my rage or that I felt cheated out of the life Scott and I had envisioned. We'd traveled the world, embraced adventures, and stayed physically active now, everything had changed. I was tangled in a whirlwind of anger and gratitude, grateful that Scott was still here but seething at the drastic turn our life had taken.

Fortunately, my therapist was no rookie. She expertly guided me through the process, helping me tackle the feelings I'd been avoiding. She had this uncanny ability to help me see things from a fresh perspective. What I didn't expect was that she'd be on my side first, last, and always. Even while empathizing with Scott's health struggles, her focus was on *me*. I hadn't realized how angry I truly was until she helped me see that it was okay to feel pissed off about what was happening, not just to Scott but to me. Yes, it was happening to me too. Coming to that realization was tough, but I got there, and slowly, my anger began to fade. Letting go of it felt transformative. Sure, I still felt sad and disappointed, but I could finally release that lingering emotion that was, as they say, "no longer serving me."

I started to sleep better, figure out ways to move forward, and look for bright spots. And there were many. I had amazing running friends who were there to support me for all my training runs, whether it involved hills, track, or long runs. Scott's health began to slowly improve. He was eating more by mouth and getting some weight back on. We had hit rock bottom, and we were climbing out together.

Chapter 10 – Boston, By Way of Idaho 2020

I n the summer of 2020, COVID-19 dragged on with the world and our country constantly arguing about whether it was a pandemic, serious, not serious, a cold, a flu, or a death sentence. Lots of opinions were espoused in the echo chambers of the internet. It was all anyone talked about even before the vaccine controversy started. In late May, the Boston Athletic Association (BAA) announced that they would have a virtual race in September 2020. We would receive our race packets and goodies in a "pre-race" box; we could run anywhere we wanted, upload our time to their website, and later receive a finisher box that would include our medal. Ideal? No.

Many people hesitated to commit to a virtual race, but I had kept up my running, taking only a brief break to grieve when the marathon was canceled. I decided to go ahead with the virtual race, determined to still chase a personal best. I had trained hard and was in solid marathon shape. I reconnected with Coach Rhonda, who helped me craft a new plan, and once again, I found myself training through the sweltering summer heat for a September marathon.

With gyms closed, I devised strength workouts at home, tuned into virtual yoga sessions with a local studio, and ran with a few friends as my training picked up speed. But as race day drew nearer, worry began to creep in. *Where could I run the marathon?* Initially, I had hoped to travel to Boston and run along the Charles River to at least capture a piece of the city's spirit, but quarantine rules and restrictions made that plan impossible.

We had a whole crew of local runners planning a virtual Boston Marathon course in Wilmington, but it was shaping up to be a hot, humid, and downright miserable experience. To make matters worse, they were all time qualifiers and way faster than me. *I don't want to run a marathon and finish an hour later than everyone else.* The thought of plodding along alone while everyone else celebrated at the finish line did not appeal. In reality, I lacked the motivation to tackle the heat and humidity in Wilmington. It felt like a recipe for a meltdown, both literally and figuratively.

After a grueling sixteen-mile training run on a sweltering Saturday in July, I headed to the beach to meet up with my college friend Barb, who had traveled all the way from Sandpoint, Idaho, to visit family in Wilmington. We go way back; college roommates, sorority sisters, and lifelong friends. But honestly, I was in a funk, grumpy, and frustrated not just from the heat, but from feeling lost in meeting my goal.

Barb took one look at my sour expression and, without missing a beat, said, "Why don't you run your marathon in Sandpoint?" I started listing all the reasons in my head why that would be a terrible idea, but then I paused and just stared at her. *What if I could run my marathon there?* Suddenly, a spark of excitement flickered in the back of my mind. Sandpoint was a beautiful place, and the thought of a change of scenery was tantalizing. I pulled out my phone to look at the current temperature there, the dew point, and the morning lows. Forty-five degrees for an overnight temperature with a very low dew point and it was July. September would be even better.

"Are you serious?" I asked her.

"Yes, I'm serious. I'm sure there is a local running group in town that can help us put a course together."

Barb was the type of person who could make things happen. She's the backbone of many friendships I've maintained since college, always rallying support and bringing people together.

As we discussed my options, I warmed up to her idea. Sandpoint would be much cooler with less humidity, and it's undeniably beautiful. I loved Sandpoint. In what seemed like five minutes, we had formulated a plan, and as soon as she returned home, Barb immediately jumped into action, rallying the local running community to help create a marathon course for me.

Sandpoint, a small town in the northern part of Idaho, is nestled between the Rocky Mountains and Lake Pend Oreille. It's a beautiful place to run, but with its two-lane roads and limited shoulders, I knew we'd have to get creative. I scoured the "Map My Run" website, analyzing elevations and potential routes, and as the day drew closer, a plan began to take shape.

Barb and our friend Debbie, a fellow sorority sister and also a local resident of Sandpoint, would follow me in the car to make sure I didn't get run over. Meanwhile, a local friend of Barb's would run and bike ahead of me to keep things safe and organized. I'd fly into Spokane, Washington, a few days before and run my race on Saturday, September 12, 2020. Suddenly, the idea that had started as a mere spark was becoming a full-fledged road map.

The plan gave me new motivation and got me through the last of my long, hot training runs. I kept thinking about those cool temps in Idaho and how great it was going to feel to run there. Barb knew everyone in Sandpoint, and soon, the word spread that I was coming from North Carolina to run a virtual Boston Marathon. I finished up the last bit of training with a spring in my step, and I was ready to put my fitness and nutrition to the test.

I arrived in Spokane, and immediately, someone from the local newspaper called and wanted to interview me about the virtual marathon. While Barb drove the hour and a half to Sandpoint, I answered the reporter's questions on the phone. I talked about the fundraising experience, explained why I chose Sandpoint, and where I planned to finish. They wanted to be there to get a photo.

Local runner Carol also planned to run her virtual marathon the day after mine. She was featured in the same article. Amazingly, she didn't start running marathons until she was in her sixties but she was so successful that she earned sponsorships and had already run in Boston several times. She wanted to come to my finish line and be a part of the celebration, and I had planned to return the favor.

I started carb-loading three days before the big day, guzzling electrolytes like they were the nectar of the gods. I also made a concerted effort to keep my feet up as much as possible before race day. The weather couldn't have been better, with perfect, sunny, blue skies and no humidity, with morning lows in the 40s. The air felt cool and crisp. Perfect for running.

The day before the race, Barb and I drove the course. Unknown to her team, they'd even managed to sneak in some hills around mile fifteen, similar to the Boston Newtown hills on the course. And just as we were getting ready for the finish, they had me slated to switch to a gravel trail. We quickly modified that section since I didn't want to transition from road to gravel so late in the race. Barb and Debbie set up a finish line by the lake for me, complete with friends and the local newspaper photographer to capture the moment. Debbie would be my timekeeper, while Barb drove the car with a giant "Runner Ahead" poster on the back. Everything felt perfect.

I came across a quote by Anita Sands that resonated with me the night before my run: "Remember, you don't need a certain number of friends, just a number of friends you can be certain of." Barb and Debbie were definitely those friends. Solid and supportive every step of the way.

I went to bed Friday night fully carb-loaded, feeling prepared mentally and physically to tackle the marathon. I cracked the window in the bedroom to let in the fresh air. Around midnight, I woke up to an unusual smell. Smoke. At first, I thought I was dreaming, but as I inhaled again, the harsh, acrid scent was undeniable. Wildfires had been raging across the Pacific Northwest for weeks, but Sandpoint had remained untouched, a safe haven from the devastation. *You have got to be kidding me.*

That night, the wind shifted, and by dawn, the air thickened with smoke, an oppressive haze that clung to everything. It wasn't just the smell it was the taste in the back of my throat. The conditions I'd hoped for the crisp, cool morning air that would carry me through the miles had vanished. Instead, a toxic cloud enveloped the landscape, threatening my health, my lungs, and the race I had worked so hard for. This wasn't how it was supposed to go. But here I was, staring at a marathon that had just become a whole lot harder.

I had no experience with wildfires or air quality indexes. Wind directions, smoke maps, and the risks of inhaling toxic air were foreign concepts to me. But honestly, none of that mattered. I was determined to run this marathon, smoke-filled air be damned. I threw on my charity singlet, laced up my shoes, and we headed to the start area. I Facetimed Scott so he could see me at the start line, a bittersweet moment. I wished that he could be there with me. But as dawn broke, it was go time.

I put in my AirPods and started a Rich Roll podcast, the one where he interviewed Des Linden about her Boston Marathon win. Des shared so many epic insights and fueled my motivation as I hit the pavement. Alyn, a local triathlete, ran just ahead of me in comfortable silence. Debbie and Barb were my personal hydration team, handing me water and gels when I needed them. Meanwhile, the air quality kept getting worse, but we all pretended it was just an unusually cloudy day. When I crossed the long bridge spanning the lake, I could barely make out the water through the haze. Barb and Debbie were monitoring the air quality index, but they never suggested we stop. I was relieved; I didn't want to quit. Not today. Not after all the planning and heart that had gone into this marathon.

At the twenty-mile mark, I felt good. Really good. I started smiling ear to ear. I was going to run a personal best. I knew it. I had never felt this good at twenty miles. I had no GI issues. No bathroom was needed at mile sixteen or seventeen. No monkey on my back at mile eighteen. My legs felt good, and despite the air quality, my lungs felt good as well. In my bones, I knew I was having a breakthrough moment in my marathon experience.

Alyn switched to biking a few feet in front of me, and another local runner joined me with a couple of miles left to go. She tried to talk to me, but I didn't want to listen or respond, so I put on some fast, classic rock music and pushed. I saw a small gathering of people at a finish line area on the lake. I raised my arms in the air, a huge smile on my face. When my watch clicked over 26.2 miles, I had finished my fourth marathon in 4:39:28. I was forty-one minutes faster than Berlin, three minutes faster than London, and ecstatic. I had run the kind of marathon I knew I could. The conditions weren't perfect, but it was far better than hot and humid Wilmington.

Amazing, lifelong friends stood by my side, and new friendships blossomed along the way. That day turned out to be one of the best. Barb and Debbie, the real deal, along with their friends, made the experience even more special. Although the time wouldn't officially count since the course wasn't US Track and Field certified and didn't contribute to the Six Star Medal, hitting the 4:30s just slightly felt like a major victory. The run had been executed flawlessly, and once again, valuable lessons were learned. Confidence soared.

Carol, the local runner doing her virtual marathon the next day, even came to my finish line to congratulate me, which touched me so much. Once finished, I called Coach Rhonda and Scott, crying (again), and took lots of selfies.

I sat contemplating how I was ever going to walk again when my new friend Rachel asked, "Do you want to take an Epsom salt bath in the birthing center? We have huge bathtubs." Rachel worked at a midwifery clinic just down the street.

"Mumm, okay," I said, unsure about the idea but also thinking it might be a heavenly way to soothe my sore muscles. I had never been to a birthing center before, so my curiosity was peaked. We drove about five minutes to the clinic, and Rachel started filling a gigantic tub with warm water, setting out towels, and lighting candles.

"I will wash your hair for you and help you get in," she said while she moved around the space. I stood in my sweaty running clothes, not sure what to do, thinking she would leave to let me get undressed and into the tub. "Go ahead and get in when you're ready," she said.

I felt more than a little self-conscious. But Rachel was used to dealing with naked pregnant women in labor and thought nothing of privacy.

"To hell with it," I said and began peeling off my sweaty gear before stepping into the tub.

"I'm so sorry, you might've wanted some privacy! I didn't even think about it." We both laughed. Before long, Barb and Debbie came in while Rachel pampered me, turning the moment into an impromptu celebration. Rachel, who was pregnant herself, kept the energy light and fun, with discussions about quirky baby names and the events of the day. Despite having just met her the day before, she had such a calm, kind presence, making me feel completely at ease. I had seen her cheering on the course with her husband during my race, which meant the world to me.

In that moment, I truly felt cared for by these wonderful women, by the support of the community, and by myself, for allowing others to take care of me when I needed it most. Volunteers at local races always earn my gratitude, but during a virtual run, their support felt even more meaningful. A local runner had made me a "Boston Virtual Marathon" finisher medal, which I wore proudly all day. That day wasn't just about crossing the finish line, it was about the love and kindness I felt along the way.

Afterward, we headed back to Barb's house and ordered food while I stretched and did yoga poses. Later, we gathered as a group for dinner and celebrated the day and the accomplishments of everyone involved. Barb had helped fulfill this dream, and her friends were now my friends. We laughed, toasted, and feasted. I couldn't stop smiling, thinking about the town, the people, and the day.

Sandpoint will forever hold a special place in my heart. It's not just the stunning scenery; it's the friendly, supportive people who make it feel like home. This "race" changed my running going forward. I dialed in nutrition and training and saw the results. I felt proud of myself for going forward to "race" this marathon and have a "finish." I needed to put Boston to bed until it was time to wake it up again. It wasn't long until we started to see a glimmer of hope that the historic Boston Marathon would make a comeback and in the most unique way.

Boston by way of Idaho, September 12, 2020

Chapter 11 – Boston Training 2.0

O ur beloved poodle Toby died on Thanksgiving 2020. We were crushed to lose him at fourteen years old. Just one more awful thing to happen during the pandemic. To cheer up, Scott and I went to Destin, Florida, for Christmas. We stayed in a beach condo, rode bikes, and mostly kept to ourselves. Unfortunately, upon our return, Scott contracted COVID-19. He spent three days in bed with a migraine, barely eating or drinking. I also tested positive, but my symptoms were relatively mild, limited to fatigue and the frustrating loss of taste and smell.

During his bout with coronavirus, Scott began losing weight at an alarming rate, struggling to eat enough to sustain himself. I hadn't noticed how much weight he had lost since I was with him every day, but during a follow-up appointment with his surgeon, we learned he needed another feeding tube immediately. It was a tough blow, as we thought those days were behind us, but it was also a blessing that such solutions were available to help patients regain their strength. About six months after recovering from COVID-19, I started to experience heart palpitations and occasional chest pain, but only after running, of course, because that's how these plot twists work. I consulted a cardiologist and went through a thorough examination, complete with an EKG and chest X-rays, all of which came back normal. Great news, right? Except that after a few months, my palpitations decided to throw a farewell party, only to be replaced by sudden spikes in heart rate.

I'd be jogging along at a moderate pace, heart rate around 135, and then boom! Suddenly, I was in a 200-beats-per-minute dance-off with my own heart. I'd have to stop and walk like I'd just sprinted a 5K while carrying a refrigerator. My chest felt weird, not tight like I was having a heart attack, but *off*. The moment I stopped running, it would act like nothing happened, as if it was just trying to keep things exciting. This went on for eighteen frustrating months. Some runs were fine, even during high-intensity tempo workouts. But then, out of nowhere, my heart would decide to spike like it was auditioning for a role in an action movie. It was both perplexing and frustrating.

I couldn't pinpoint this issue to specific foods, but I did notice a connection with alcohol, particularly wine and beer. Just one glass the night before a run could send my heart rate on a rollercoaster ride. So, I made the decision to abstain from alcohol before my runs, which helped a bit (I know, I couldn't believe I abstained either). However, this issue lingered throughout 2021 and a good chunk of 2022. It added a layer of anxiety to every run, especially during races. It felt like there was always something else to contend with, turning my training into an obstacle course.

Combine all of this with losing our dog, and I think we can all agree that 2020 was a horrific year that just wouldn't end. In a bid to bring some much-needed joy into our lives, we did the COVID thing and adopted a rescue dog. We affectionately named him Bodie, after legendary skier Bode Miller. The main motivation was to have a running buddy. Bodie, a Jack Russell mutt, turned out to be a natural runner. He was a breeze to train and quickly became an enthusiastic participant in our group runs, fully embracing his role in our pack. Bodie brought a new level of joy and fun to my running experience. He wasn't just a beloved member of the running community; he was a source of endless happiness at home.

Scott was still navigating the healing process with his jaw. He had recovered from all the infections but was still dealing with high levels of pain from the trigeminal nerve. The feeding tube was helping him gain weight, which relieved some of the pressure of needing to eat enough to maintain weight. Having Bodie around helped him cope with the pain and got him outside for daily walks. Scott was most at peace in the woods, and those walks with Bodie brought him much-needed happiness.

As time passed, Bodie's endurance grew, and he began running longer distances with us. Before we knew it, he was comfortably keeping pace for ten-mile runs. Running with Bodie became a sanctuary, providing an anchor during those days when the ongoing challenges of the COVID-19 pandemic threatened to make me crazy. I also worried that my quest for the World Marathon Majors might fall apart if the Boston Athletic Association (BAA) didn't offer us another chance to run the Boston Marathon.

Shortly after the virtual Boston Marathon race, smaller local races began to make a comeback. At the start of 2021, there was hope that COVID-19 would become a thing of the past. However, the number of cases continued to rise as more people contracted the virus.

As the year progressed, discussions bubbled up within our running community about the BAA's plans for those of us who, after raising significant funds for various charities, had participated in the virtual Boston Marathon. Many of us felt we had missed out on the quintessential Boston experience, and if the BAA intended to hold an in-person race in 2021, they needed to consider not only the qualifying runners but also those who ran in support of charities. This sentiment prompted me to write a heartfelt letter to the BAA outlining my perspective.

In my letter, I highlighted that I had raised over $8,500 for charity and was eager to train again to complete the race in person in Boston. While I understood that the BAA legally didn't owe us anything, I hoped to appeal to them as fellow human beings. As a collective, the charity runners had raised over $27 million, and we felt we were an important part of the race. There was considerable debate online about Boston qualifiers versus charity runners and who "deserved" to be there more. The race caps at around thirty-six thousand runners, making every spot highly coveted. The BAA sets aside a specific number of entries for charity runners, along with spots for qualifiers, corporate entries, and other random participants. Many would-be qualifiers feel that charity runners are "stealing" their chances of running the race. I suspected the debate would continue as it got harder to qualify for this marathon.

Eventually, the BAA made the eagerly awaited announcement that there would indeed be an in-person marathon in 2021. However, it came with a significant twist. The race would take place in October, a stark deviation from its usual date on the third Monday in April, Patriots' Day. This change was necessitated by ongoing restrictions on large gatherings due to the pandemic. Despite the uncertainty, the news of the forthcoming Boston Marathon, the world's oldest marathon, was met with unbridled enthusiasm. I felt relieved and hopeful that my quest for the Six Star Medal was still alive.

Around this time, I received an unexpected message from my charity offering me a coveted entry for the race with one condition. I needed to raise an additional $4,000. The thought of gathering that substantial sum during a pandemic was formidable. Many people were struggling with unemployment, and times were undeniably tough. Could I muster the energy and resources for yet another fundraising effort? The idea felt physically and emotionally draining. Walking away at this stage also felt like an unthinkable betrayal of all the effort and commitment I had already put into this cause. Boston Marathon entries were fiercely competitive, and fundraising was no different. With an entry already reserved for me, I knew I had to see this through.

I started brainstorming how to raise the funds. I felt terrible asking my friends, family, and coworkers for more money. I knew I sounded like a broken record, and I needed a new approach. Our local running store, Fleet Feet, had a program where they collected used athletic shoes to donate to those in need worldwide. For charity organizations that donated a significant quantity of shoes, they offered cash based on weight.

I called my friend, Michelle, who owns our local Fleet Feet, and asked if I could use this idea to raise money for Boston. She agreed, and I hatched a plan. I would encourage people to donate their running shoes, tennis shoes, pickleball shoes, and any other athletic footwear they could spare. Soon, people began cleaning out their closets, their kids' closets, and even their spouses' closets. This initiative served a dual purpose: not only did it enable me to amass a substantial collection of shoes for those in need, but it also raised awareness for my Boston fundraising efforts. Shoes and donations started pouring in from my incredible network of friends, family, and colleagues.

I won't sugarcoat it: the process was arduous. I was constantly driving to people's houses to pick up shoes or receiving drop-offs at my home. Neighbors, friends, friends of friends, family, and even complete strangers I had never met before all joined in to contribute to the cause. I set a clear goal to raise $4,000 well in advance of the deadline and established milestones to keep me on track. Once again, I recognized that moving forward inch by inch was the only way to make it happen.

Given the October race date, I faced the prospect of another summer training program, and I dreaded it, forever rolling my eyes at the thought of training in the North Carolina summer. I knew substantial changes to create a more conducive training environment were necessary to help both mentally and physically. That's when I decided to work with Coach Jen. I explained my heart rate issues, my physical challenges primarily involving my pesky knee (throwback to that high school ski trip), and my concern about training in the heat. Together, we devised a training program that included tempo and hill runs; we also incorporated tempo segments into my long runs. Coach Jen helped me establish a schedule for the much-needed rest days, which I was notoriously bad at taking. She emphasized the importance of stretching and strength training. I had already built a solid running base early in the year and had the support of a trainer at my local gym to improve my overall strength, particularly in my left knee, the one I had injured skiing all those years ago.

Many other locals were gearing up to run the October Boston Marathon. My friend Kevin reached out to me through Facebook and mentioned he was also running for charity. It was the perfect opportunity for us to team up and train together. One early morning run, as the sun was just starting to rise, we were headed toward the beach, bleary-eyed and half-asleep. That's when Kevin broached the idea of going to Boston for an extended training run. I was immediately interested, but I couldn't shake off concerns about the expenses: airfare, accommodations, and all the costs associated with a weekend trip.

There was an active Boston Charity Runner Facebook community that met every Saturday in downtown Boston for long runs on the actual Boston Marathon course. As I viewed their updates and pictures on Facebook, I felt the familiar pang of FOMO wash over me. I found out Kevin had an equal dose of FOMO; we were kindred spirits in this way. Then, Kevin dropped a bomb that completely caught me off guard.

"We could fly to Boston for the weekend and do the charity group training run. And we can take my jet," he said.

"As in a private jet?" I chuckled.

"Yeah, we can take my jet up to Boston Friday, carb-load in the North End, meet the Charity group and run on Saturday,

178

and come back Sunday." He said it like having access to a jet was the most normal thing in the world.

I mean, of course, yes! I did have a brief thought: Am I about to be kidnapped and my kidneys sold to the highest bidder? Then, I found out Colin was going too. A meteorologist for a local TV station, he was the perfect candidate for a dramatic rescue. If he got snatched, everyone would be scrambling to find him and by default, I'd probably get swept up in the search. Who could resist a high-stakes, TV-worthy rescue when a weather guy goes missing?

Kevin worked fast, and soon we had a plan in motion. Seven of us would fly to Boston on a Friday, complete a seventeen-mile run on Saturday with the charity group, and return home on Sunday. I was 100 percent on board with this extraordinary plan.

A few weeks later, Kevin's plane lifted off, filled with laughter and selfies. While not my first time flying in a private plane, this marked the first purely fun trip. Conversations about running flowed easily as we cruised up the coast. Normally, I harbored a fear of flying in small planes, but the weather cooperated, and as we approached Boston, we had stunning aerial views of the city and harbor.

Kevin had rented a couple of cars for our trip, and soon he was navigating the city's notoriously hectic streets. I admit there were moments when I had to close my eyes. We checked into our hotel and started walking around. Our first order of business was to visit the famous Boston Marathon finish line painted on Boylston Street. As we posed for selfies, a man in a parked car started yelling at us, thinking we were taking pictures of him. He decided to grace us with a profanity-laden welcome to Boston. We had only been in the city for an hour, and we were already getting cursed out by locals.

We decided to indulge in serious carb-loading in Boston's famous North End at a fantastic Italian restaurant. This part of Boston should be a requirement when visiting the city. There were so many great restaurants, mostly Italian, and the architecture made me feel like I was in a European city. It was a perfect evening, and it seemed like everyone was out on the streets. After dinner, we stopped at a staple in the North End, Mike's Pastry, for their famous cannoli. I loved the atmosphere. As we headed back to the hotel, Kevin and I couldn't pass up the opportunity to swing by the Cheers bar for a quick brew and soak up the ambiance of this famous watering hole. Boston has so many great restaurants, neighborhoods, and historical sites, and I couldn't wait to see it all.

The next morning, we joined the charity running group for the scheduled run from the Prudential Center. We found ourselves surrounded by friends from the Facebook group, preparing to run on the hallowed Boston Marathon course. We started at the finish line and headed back toward Hopkinton, where the race would start. The landmarks along the historic course were both inspiring and surreal. I found it hard to believe I was on the path to running the Boston Marathon, a race with a storied history that countless talented men and women have participated in, and where the revolution of women's marathoning was born.

It was a scorching day for our long run, but the heat didn't faze us. We wore smiles and quickly realized that the notorious Heartbreak Hill was no laughing matter. Fortunately, the Boston Fire Department was stationed at the top of the hill, offering us much-needed cold towels, potato chips, and words of encouragement. During the run, I also had the chance to meet my friend Michael, a fellow user of Strava, a social network and app for runners and athletes. Michael, a dedicated runner and father, has been a great source of inspiration to me throughout the years. Meeting him in person and sharing a heartfelt hug was a highlight of the run.

Kevin and I had an amazing training run despite the hot day, and we loved meeting all our Facebook friends in person. After we cleaned up, we grabbed a quick lunch, which, of course, included a "lobsta" roll. Then we headed back to the Prudential Center and the Under Armor store to shop and use the NormaTec boots, which were a compression technology for helping our legs recover after a long training session. We felt like rock stars lounging in recliners, getting our legs rejuvenated. Kevin loved Boston, which made it fun for me to see the sights and experience his favorite places.

The next day, our group gathered for a short recovery run around Boston Common and along the Charles River. It was a fitting way to conclude our incredible weekend. The trip was a perfect blend of friends, delicious food, and invigorating runs, making it truly a perfect experience. To be honest, it felt like one of the high points of my life. I couldn't contain my excitement at the prospect of returning in a few months to run the actual Boston Marathon course.

As the months rolled by and the race date loomed ever closer, it seemed increasingly likely that the marathon would indeed take place. At last, the reality began to set in: we were on the brink of actually running the Boston Marathon. A dream that was about to become a thrilling reality. I traveled back and forth to the North Carolina mountains to run at elevation and in cooler temperatures. I did countless hill repeats across the Topsail Island bridge forty minutes north of my house to prepare for the hilly Boston course. The Boston Marathon, considered a net downhill course, presented a series of challenging hills starting at mile seventeen, also known as the Newton Hills, which culminate at mile twenty on Heartbreak Hill. My goal was to be well-prepared for these late-race challenges, both mentally and physically.

In mid-September, I completed my final twenty-mile-long run at Topsail Island, repeatedly traversing up and over the bridge to fine-tune my elevation training. I was ready to start tapering to ensure my muscles would be well-rested and capable of handling the full distance. All I had left to do was hydrate, rest, carb-load, and run the Boston Marathon.

Chapter 12 – Boston Marathon 2021

Recording videos of myself felt awkward, and sometimes even made me a little queasy. I think most people feel that way discomfort with the way we sound or look on camera. For me, it wasn't just about the awkwardness of speaking into a lens; I felt like I had to make myself look "presentable" hair done, makeup on, the whole deal just to ask people to donate to my charity. I cringed when those videos popped up in my Facebook memories, but they served a purpose. Despite the awkwardness, the contributions from my friends, family, and generous strangers helped me meet the fundraising goal required to run the Boston Marathon.

In total, I raised over $12,500. When I think about that number now, I'm awestruck. The generosity of others, the belief they had in me and the cause, humbled me in ways I couldn't fully appreciate until much later. Once again, it wasn't just about crossing a finish line; it was about the community that supported me and the people who helped me realize this dream. Whenever I found myself facing a tough run or doubting my ability to finish the training cycle, all I had to do was remember the kindness and generosity of the people around me. It put everything in perspective. In those moments of struggle, I realized how lucky and fortunate I truly am. The support I received wasn't just a financial boost; it was a reminder that there's a whole network of people behind me, cheering me on every step of the way. And that's something extremely incredible.

My training partners, Mike, Tracy, and Dee, whom I affectionately refer to as my "BRFs" (Best Running Friends), joined me on countless hilly runs, track workouts, and long runs, even on those swelteringly humid days. They were so generous with their time and selfless in their willingness to run with me no matter what I had on the plan. The day before my departure for Boston, we went for a short shakeout run, and afterward, we shared our last coffee meetup, reminiscing about all our training runs.

Scott had finally started to recover from his bout of COVID-19. His weight was back up, and we formulated a plan to maintain it through supplemental protein shakes. His swallowing improved slightly, which allowed for the removal of the feeding tube. Having him in a healthier mental and physical state was a major relief. Scott decided to stay back and take care of the dogs while I went and fulfilled this long-awaited dream. It saddened me that he wouldn't be there, but he needed to focus on his own health and well-being and not be traversing the streets of Boston to take care of me after the race.

My friend Susan accompanied me, acting as my helper, offering companionship, logistical support, and moral encouragement for Marathon Monday. Her friends, Ron and Roberta, lived in Brookline, a suburb of Boston, close to the Boston Marathon course, and generously opened their home to us for the weekend. They not only offered their hospitality but also prepared meals and provided me with their son's room. Their beautiful home was conveniently located within walking distance to Boston's subway system, the "T," making it easy to access the city.

Upon our arrival in Boston, I wasted no time and headed straight to the expo to collect my race packet, take photos at the finish line area, and immerse myself in the marathon atmosphere. The expo was a bit disappointing; it was small, with only a few vendors and no elite marathon speakers. However, there was a big wall displaying all the participants names. I found my name and snapped a photo. For this race, we had to prove we were vaccinated or take a COVID test in one tent before moving to the expo area. It wasn't as fun as a normal race expo, but at least we were there. The finish line area was packed with runners taking photos and chatting about how ready we were to run this historic race.

Drawing from the lessons learned during my race experience in Berlin, I decided to limit my walking and sightseeing in Boston. That morning, Susan and I visited the Isabella Stewart Gardner Museum, an art museum modeled after a Venetian palazzo, and that afternoon, I took a Boston Duck Tour, which offered sightseeing on land and water with a bus that turned into a boat. The rest of the day was spent with my feet up, eating carbs, and drinking water.

On Sunday, the charity team organized a brunch featuring Boston Marathon and New York City Marathon champion and Olympic silver medalist in the marathon, Meb Keflezighi, a true legend and national treasure. Also, long-time Boston Marathon director Dave McGillivray was in attendance, speaking and answering questions about the Boston Marathon experience. Kevin and I were starstruck and inspired by these great men. I had the privilege of meeting Meb and there was no way I could pass up the chance for a photo with him. Meb truly exemplifies running with a positive mindset, and I felt like I had met an American hero that day. He gave us lots of pointers on how to run the Boston Marathon (don't go out too fast) and reminded us to enjoy the experience, take it all in, and realize we're making history running the 125th Boston Marathon in October, which had never been done before.

From 1897 until 1968, the Boston Marathon had taken place on April 19, Patriots' Day, a holiday commemorating the start of the Revolutionary War, but this changed in April 1969 when Patriots' Day officially became the third Monday in April. There are only two other times when it was not held on Patriots' Day. One was in April 2020 due to the pandemic when it was canceled and moved to a virtual race, and the other was in 2021, when it was held on October 11 due to quarantine restrictions in April.

Dave McGillivray, race Director of the Boston Marathon since 2001 and seasoned runner in his own right, shared his insights into the extensive process of organizing such an iconic race, highlighting his many years of dedication. One particularly impressive tradition was his annual marathon run on the course after the last runner had crossed the finish line. This commitment underscores his passion for the Boston Marathon. Kevin and I sat next to each other googly-eyed, as I'm sure many other runners did as well, over these amazing men who were so much a part of the history of the Boston

Marathon. The room was dead quiet while the two of them talked of their running careers and what this race meant to them.

After brunch, the rest of the day was dedicated to race preparation. I spent time reading, stretching, foam rolling, spoiling Ron and Roberta's dog, Trevor, and, as expected, filling up on carbohydrates. I had warned Ron and Roberta that my carb-loading might "shock and awe" them. Ron prepared a fantastic pre-race meal of chicken and rice while Susan and I created a race meetup plan, both on the course and at the finish line. Susan planned to be at mile seventeen to hand me nutrition and provide moral support. We'd meet again at the finish line.

The Boston Marathon course was a point-to-point route from Hopkinton to downtown Boston. Hopkinton, known for nothing more than being the start line for the race and 26.2 miles from Boston, looked to be a typical quaint New England town. Cape Cod homes, brick churches, and a tree-lined park in the center of town. Thankfully, the charity teams had arranged a bus to take us to the start line, so we didn't have to navigate getting there from downtown Boston.

The next morning, I met up with Kevin and his family at the bus stop downtown, where we hugged and said our goodbyes to his wife and kids before boarding the bus to Hopkinton. It was finally "go time!"

Upon arrival, I began to feel a sense of anticipation and excitement that sent chills down my spine. I wanted to savor every moment of the experience. During the bus ride, I met a doctor from Texas who was running her first marathon. Despite having just met, we instantly bonded, sharing our enthusiasm. Kevin and I planned to run together for as long as possible, with no pressure to keep up if one of us felt stronger and wanted to go faster. Our strategy was to start slowly, knowing that Boston's course has a history of tempting runners to go out too fast at the beginning, particularly with its significant downhill portions that can unknowingly strain the quadriceps.

Due to COVID-19 precautions, there wasn't an official start time for our wave. We were simply instructed to walk up and begin when we felt ready. Kevin and I shed our throwaway clothes, and after a visit to the porta-johns, we took a few photos with our new doctor friend. We discussed all the runners who had stood at this very spot before us. I was determined to cherish every minute of this unique experience, fully aware that it would pass by all too quickly. Tears pricked my eyes as I thought about Roberta Gibb, Kathrine Switzer, and countless others who were denied the chance to run this race because they were women.

Roberta (Bobbi) Gibb made history in 1966 as the first woman to run the Boston Marathon. However, she couldn't just sign up like the other runners since women were not allowed to race. It was thought that our organs would fall out or other such nonsense. Instead, she hid in the bushes to avoid detection by race officials and jumped into the race after it started. Her determination was a quiet defiance of the gender barriers in place at the time.

Then, in 1967, Kathrine Switzer made her own stand. When she registered for the Boston Marathon, she cleverly used her initials instead of her full name, hoping to pass as male. She received a race bib and officially entered the race. However, when officials saw her running, they tried to physically remove her from the course. What happened next became one of the most iconic moments in marathon history. Switzer's boyfriend, a burly man, body-slammed the race official to protect her, and Switzer finished the race as the first woman to officially complete the Boston Marathon. Her act of defiance sparked a movement and challenged the outdated idea that women didn't belong in long-distance races.

It wasn't until 1972, however, that women were officially allowed to participate in the Boston Marathon. That year, eight women ran, and all of them finished, marking the beginning of a new era in the sport. They broke barriers for so many incredible female athletes who have since run on this hallowed course but also for ordinary runners like me who wanted to be a part of history.

I reflected on all the effort that had brought me to this moment. Three years of training for Boston, a virtual marathon in Idaho, countless miles logged, and more electrolytes sweated out than I cared to think about. There were the carb-loading sessions, where rice and quinoa became as familiar as old friends, and two years of dedicated fundraising. I'd put in the work, pushed through the doubts, and now was the time. All those early mornings, the pain, the sacrifices, the tears, the disappointment, the thrill of knowing I would get to run after all it all led to this. I was more than ready.

Cool, humid weather kicked off the race but quickly progressed to a muggy, mid-sixties day. Although I'd much prefer drizzle and forty-five degrees, I was at the Boston Marathon, and nothing was going to dampen my enthusiasm. With a burst of excitement, Kevin and I hit "start" on our watches and began running side by side, soaking in the sights, a huge smile plastered on my face. I was living my dream!

Starting out, we closely monitored our watches and deliberately kept a slow pace. The course ran downhill for the first five miles and felt incredibly easy. We zipped through towns where spectators lined the streets, ringing cowbells, clapping, and cheering for us. We waved and smiled at everyone, feeling the incredible support from the crowd. As the course started to flatten out, we continued running comfortably, keeping our pace in mind. We did mental body scans, asking each other how we felt. Kevin mentioned a minor issue with his leg, and I had a little concern with my foot and toe, but overall, we felt great and kept taking in the sights and relishing the fact that we were running the Boston Marathon.

We spotted fellow Wilmington running friends on the course, along with Kevin's family cheering us on. Before long, we began to hear the unmistakable roar of the "scream tunnel" in Wellesley. Wellesley College was famous for its spirited and loud female spectators who traditionally offer kisses to passing runners. While kisses weren't a wise choice during COVID-19, we encountered hilarious signs and memorable moments, including two famous Boston golden retrievers who were there for the photo ops. Around this time, I tried to take some photos with my phone, but it started making weird noises and locking up, rendering it completely unusable. Unable to play music, snap pictures, or do anything but stare in frustration, I decided to put it away and focus on the run. I grabbed Gatorade at nearly every aid station and fueled up every forty-five minutes. I was feeling good, even if a few areas felt a little off during my mental body scan. I didn't want to dwell on the negatives, so I kept smiling and waving.

As we approached mile seventeen, I spotted my friend Susan on the course. It felt amazing to see a friendly face cheering me on. Kevin had fallen a bit behind me, and though I was unsure where he was, I heard his voice reassuring Susan that I was doing well. I felt a mix of concern for him but relief that he was still nearby. I knew the hills starting at this mile mark were going to be tough.

The Newton Hills are a series of inclines starting around mile seventeen leading to the infamous "Heartbreak Hill," a hundred-foot incline at mile twenty. Heartbreak Hill got its name in the fortieth annual running of the marathon when Boston favorite John Kelley was passed by Ellison "Tarzan" Brown at mile twenty. Brown went on to win the race, which broke Kelley's heart. The hill forever became known as Heartbreak Hill.

Switching to a run/walk strategy to conserve energy for a strong finish, I reminded myself that the famous race car driver Danica Patrick once called Heartbreak Hill "home free hill." Once over that hill, we'd be home free into Boston. Sure, there were still six miles to go, but any seasoned marathoner will tell you a marathon is just a twenty-mile warm-up for a six-mile race.

Kevin disappeared from sight, but a quick prayer went up for him. A strange, cramp-like pain tightened in my left inner thigh. It was a new sensation, one that caught me off guard. Hydrating with Gatorade at every aid station hadn't worked, so I switched to water, downing several cups quickly. The pain eased slightly, but the real focus shifted to staying in the moment, keeping my mind anchored to the mile at hand. Panic had no place here. I reminded myself that anxiety wouldn't help, not after the lessons learned in Berlin. Adjusting the strategy felt empowering one step at a time, one mile at a time, keeping the mind clear and the body moving.

The discomfort in my leg subsided, but a new problem emerged my right big toe. *Fantastic*. Exactly what I needed. The toe throbbed, and I quickly realized it was affecting my running form, which was likely the source of the pain in my left leg. No time for self-pity. Push through, press on. Conquer this, and the medal would be mine, with bragging rights to boot.

The first Newton Hill loomed like Everest, but somehow, I made it up without passing out. The rest of the elevation gain wasn't easy, but nothing felt impossible after that. Danica had been right once past Heartbreak Hill, the worst was over.

As I ran through Cambridge and entered Brookline, the familiar sights stirred a new surge of energy. The giant Citgo sign and the "Boston Strong" banner on the Bowker Overpass reminded me that I'd run this route before and could do it again. *Take in the sights, stay in the moment. This is the Boston Marathon!* The rolling hills in this stretch felt like mountains, but I told myself just keep moving forward.

Once we were within the Boston city limits, spectators yelled, "Welcome to Boston!" so loudly that my ears rang, but it brought a huge smile to my face and tears to my eyes. I was officially in the Boston city limits. I was on the cusp of becoming a Boston Marathon finisher, and it was a surreal reality. This was truly happening.

The next landmark was the famous right turn onto Hereford Street, and as I made the turn, I spotted Susan taking video and cheering for me. If only the video matched the way I *felt*, like a Nike athlete, effortlessly gliding along the road. In reality? My arms barely swung, and I looked less like a graceful gazelle and more like a penguin on a mission.

Hereford Street had a slight incline that resembled scaling a mountain. Every step was a reminder of just how much effort it took to get here. But then, the infamous left turn onto Boylston Street awaited. The sight of it took my breath away. Boylston was a huge road with tens of thousands of people cheering all the way to the finish line. The roar of the crowd hit me like a wave, and I couldn't stop grinning. Tears streamed down my face as I looked at thousands of spectators packed in the streets, cheering with an intensity I could only describe as *Taylor Swift concert level*.

One particular detail provided some much-needed comic relief: a guy next to me, clad in nothing but an American flag Speedo, running with all the confidence in the world. Absurd? Absolutely. But in that moment, it added to the wild energy of it all. The crowd's enthusiasm was electric, and I soaked it up, feeling like they were all there just for me. Running down Boylston Street the place where so many legends had run before me was a moment I'll never forget. Crossing that famous finish line seemed both extremely fast and incredibly slow. In an instant, the race was over, but the memories of it would stay with me forever.

I had immense pride in myself for sticking to my goal. I thought about everyone who had supported my charities, trained with me, and helped me along the way. I crossed the finish line with a time of 4:44:45, overjoyed! Boston was a challenging course, and the weather had turned humid and sunny in the second half of the race, but my careful fueling, training, and coaching had paid off. And no late-race bathroom stops. I had finally conquered my intestines.

Once the medal was placed around my neck, I started to walk through the finish line area, and a wave of emotions crashed over me as well as pain and cramping. I briefly spotted my friend and nutritionist, Diana, who was struggling to walk due to severe cramps. We fist-pumped and congratulated each other. Despite the strong urge to sit down, I knew it was better to keep moving to help with the cramping.

My phone was still locked up, preventing me from sending or receiving texts or calls. My only option was to call 911, which I had inadvertently done numerous times by accident, prompting them to call me back and ask if I needed help. I was thinking, *No, but yes*. Susan and I hadn't established a solid post-race meeting plan, thinking we could text each other, but now I couldn't locate her anywhere. Tears welled up as I searched and searched for her, yearning to see a familiar face.

A volunteer race coordinator, whose name I never learned, saw my distress.

"What's wrong? Are you okay?" he asked.

"My phone is locked up and I can't find my people and I just want to call my husband!" I wailed.

Graciously, he offered me his phone and I dialed Scott's number. My voice was shaking as I explained what had happened. My phone was dead, I was lost, and I had no way to contact anyone. I asked him to try to reach Susan and let her know where I was. The waiting seemed endless. Each passing minute dragged on, stretching the situation into a slow, unbearable agony.

When the tears had run dry and the reality of the situation set in, I gave up trying to track Susan down. The subway was my next destination, and I made my way to the T station, feeling as if I were moving in slow motion. Every step down those stairs my quads betrayed me. It took every ounce of energy to keep going. Inside the subway, the world seemed to go on without me families, friends, all chatting about the race, their post-race plans, with all their excitement. And then there was me, alone, in a daze, like an outsider to a celebration I couldn't fully connect to. Tears welled up again, and I longed for a hug, some kind of comfort. But there was none. I boarded the T, surrounded by happy runners who had found their people. *I just need to get back to Ron and Roberta's house.* The train ride seemed to take forever. When I finally got off, I had to walk no, *hobble* the last stretch. My right toe throbbed with every step, but I was afraid to look at it, afraid of what I might find. My body was in a total fog, the exhaustion from the race catching up to me in waves, but somehow, I made it to the house.

Ron and Roberta greeted me with warmth and support, their happiness about my finish a small beacon in the haze of fatigue. They had already reached out to Susan, and she was on her way. Now that I wasn't completely alone, and knowing that Susan was on her way, it felt like a small relief in a sea of emotions. I wasn't sure when the fog would lift, but I knew that I had made it through the race, through the struggle, and back to the comfort of people who cared.

When I peeled off my running shoes, I discovered the mother of all blisters under the right big toenail. Years of marathon experience had taught me to always pack open-toed shoes for post-race recovery. Without them, I wouldn't have been able to leave the house. I soaked in Epsom salts, letting the warmth of the water soothe the pain. Susan and I spent the afternoon laughing about the chaos around the finish line, swapping stories, and unwinding from the madness of the day.

Kevin had rented the upstairs of a burger joint downtown for the charity runners and our Wilmington group. After some much-needed recovery soaking, stretching, and foam rolling I was ready to join the crew. We proudly donned our finisher jackets, swapped race tales, and toasted to the day with cold beers. The atmosphere was pure joy. Kevin finished shortly after me, marking his first marathon achievement. I felt profound pride for our little group. We had all faced setbacks, doubts, and challenges, but we made it through with grit and resilience.

The following day, my friend Brenda and I walked the Freedom Trail around Boston. My right foot, now dubbed "Frankentoe," made each step a little more interesting. But I wasn't about to miss the chance to explore the historic sites of the city and snap photos with my hard-earned medal. We both appreciated the warm day; grateful the marathon had been the day before. The walk helped loosen up our sore muscles as we took in the rich history and charm of Boston.

I boarded the plane to head home, reflected on my journey and the incredible progress I had made. With four of the six Abbott World Marathon Majors stars already under my belt, the finish line of my marathon journey was coming into view. The pandemic was receding, and races were beginning to come back for good. For the first time in a long while, it felt like the future held more possibility than uncertainty.

Boston had exceeded every expectation. The memories of that day the tears, the triumphs, the pain, and the joy would stay with me forever. Never in my wildest dreams did I imagine becoming a Boston Marathoner. But I had, and now, more than ever, I understood the lesson: never say never.

Boston Marathon, October 11, 2021

Chapter 13 – Why Don't You Try Swimming?

No offense to the profession, but I've never been a fan of doctors. Western medicine, in general, doesn't align with many of my core values. Doctors seem obsessed with diagnostics X-rays, MRIs, colonoscopies, mammograms, and on and on. They love running tests, prescribing medications, or suggesting surgeries. None of that appealed to me. How could I feel so strongly about avoiding all that when Western medicine had "cured" Scott? I didn't see it that way. For him, the so-called cure felt like another layer of hell. The endless treatments, surgeries, procedures, scans, drugs, and therapies left him worse off than before. It got to the point where he questioned if any of it had been worth it.

Admittedly, I'm guilty of thinking water and sleep can fix most things. When something hurts, I'd rather hydrate, rest, and hope for the best than seek out a doctor. But when the pain really starts to hit, when it's not just a fleeting ache or minor discomfort, those defenses start to crack. Even for someone like me, who'd rather avoid the doctor's office at all costs, there are moments when the pain demands attention.

After Boston, right knee pain set in immediately. It was strange since the right knee had always been my "good" knee the one I could rely on. The left knee, on the other hand, had been problematic since my teenage years after the skiing accident in high school. Despite hours spent in the gym strengthening both legs and knees, the sudden onset of pain left me puzzled. *Why now? What caused this?*

At least the blistered toe from the marathon healed quickly, but the right knee pain stuck around, hanging on like an unwanted guest. After a few more half marathons, the pain lingered, dull but constant. Deep down, I knew the issue wasn't going away. But here's the thing: runners are masters of denial. We're the world champions at ignoring pain, pushing through discomfort, and continuing on like nothing's wrong, to our detriment, of course.

Despite the nagging pain, I kept running. It wasn't until the discomfort became impossible to ignore that the truth set in: running wasn't helping. And yet, I still couldn't quite bring myself to accept that maybe, just maybe, it was time to listen to my body.

Why Don't You Try Swimming?

In February 2022, I broke down and got an MRI despite needing to take a valium beforehand because of my deep-seated fear of MRI machines. The orthopedic doctor diagnosed tears in both menisci, along with cartilage damage and a kneecap issue in the right knee. My attention span left the building as he listed all the things wrong with my knees. Internally rolling my eyes and barely containing my skepticism of anything he said, I did perk up once he mentioned surgery wasn't an option. *There! See! I'm right. These doctors can't fix me.*

"Why don't you try swimming?" the doctor said.

"Swimming? You're kidding, right?" I responded.

"Might be a good idea to switch to Triathlon," he said. "Take some pressure off the knees." Laughing, I left his office after he recommended a pain management doctor for gel injections to reduce inflammation. *Swimming . . . hilarious! That is never going to happen,* I thought. *This guy is a quack and doesn't know what he's talking about.*

However, once my laughter died down, I met with the pain management specialist. He was young and athletic-looking, which reassured me. He looked like an athlete, so I figured he would know what it's like to want to keep doing the sport you love despite having weaknesses. After an introduction and a handshake, he sat me down, leaned over me, and stared into my eyes.

"You have been abusing your body for decades. You have to stop running."

Decades? "What? No, I haven't," I sharply responded.

"Running is bad for your knees, plus you played tennis for many years. You have to stop abusing yourself."

Tears pricked my eyes, not because he made me sad but because he pissed me off. When I get angry, really angry, to my utter frustration, I cry, which makes me even more angry because I don't want to cry, I want to yell. This is not what a runner, or frankly, any athlete wants to hear. No, my eating habits hadn't always been perfect, and there had been nights of too much wine and too little sleep, but exercise remained a constant. Running began as a way to prevent slipping into the overweight zone. It wasn't like jumping out of airplanes or diving into extreme sports well, unless skiing counted. The point was, I was just running, for crying out loud.

I couldn't believe he was saying this to me, especially when he must be doing something to stay fit himself. If anything, I had taken better care of myself over the past five years. My blood pressure, heart rate, and BMI were all excellent, and every blood panel came back normal. His statements confused me, and his bedside manner left me frustrated.

Despite feeling uncomfortable with his statements and demeanor, we went ahead with the injections. They hurt. Bad. Maybe he was having an off day, or maybe that's just how he treated all his patients, but I sent him a scathing follow-up letter with honest feedback and never returned. The injections did nothing except drain my bank account by $900. I saw two more orthopedic doctors in town. One kept me waiting for over an hour, only to spend ninety seconds with me and tell me there was nothing that could be done for my knees. I walked out feeling even more disillusioned than before. Perhaps I was jaded, but at that point, I was done with orthopedics. It was time to move on. There had to be a way to keep my running dreams alive and still earn that Six Star Medal. If the traditional route wasn't going to work, I'd find another way.

What next? I kept running through the pain, just like every runner does, hoping it would eventually fade or somehow fix itself. Denial took over, and I pushed forward, telling myself to just keep going. A few days off here and there, then back at it again. Running was my addiction, my therapy, my joy, and I wasn't ready to let go. Stopping? Unthinkable.

One way to stay on the roads despite the pain was by becoming a "pacer" and helping others reach their running goals. During races, pacers maintain a steady pace per mile to help guide runners toward a specific time goal. Pacers typically run fifteen to twenty minutes slower than their usual pace, which worked perfectly for me especially when I was dealing with my knee issues. I usually ran a half marathon in two hours to two hours and ten minutes, so I'd pace the two-hour-thirty-minute group, helping others achieve what I couldn't at the time.

The group, always a blast, often included women returning after having a baby, new runners tackling their first half marathon, husbands struggling to keep up with wives in the faster one-hour-forty-five-minute group, or people coming back to running after a break. Whatever their story, pacing them became one of the most rewarding and enjoyable aspects of my running journey. I met new people, listened to their stories, and helped them reach their goals. And at the end of the race, when they smiled and said, "You helped me PR," it was the ultimate reward. There was no greater joy for me.

One of our local half marathons featured Bart Yasso, the "Mayor of Running," as the master of ceremonies. Bart has done countless races and runs across Death Valley and all seven continents, including Mt. Kilimanjaro. He wrote for *Runner's World* for many years and has also written several books. There's even a workout named after him called the Yasso 800s.

I had the opportunity to meet him at the expo before my first pacing gig. Feeling a mixture of excitement and nerves when I approached him, I asked for his advice on pacing and he couldn't have been more kind or encouraging. After our chat, he took a photo with me, signed my bib, and genuinely made me feel like I was part of the running community. His support meant so much.

The next morning, the day of the race, the pacers gathered for photos and warm-ups. As I stretched, I heard Bart's voice calling out to the crowd over the loudspeaker, and to my surprise, he gave me a shout-out and wished me luck. That small gesture meant more than he probably realized. It made me feel seen and supported as a first-time pacer.

In the years that followed, whenever Bart came to Wilmington to emcee races, he would greet me with a friendly smile and a word of encouragement. He never had to do that, but he did, and it spoke volumes about his character. He's not just a remarkable athlete he's a true gem of a person, always lifting others up and championing the sport of running in a way that feels authentic and inspiring. And, of course, I can't forget the Yasso 800s workout. Those are no joke! Thanks to his guidance and mentorship, I was able to pace my race flawlessly. The confidence I gained from his support carried me through that event and beyond, and I'll always be grateful for the role he played in shaping my journey as a runner.

The excitement of pacing half marathons and watching others smash their goals created a desire to do something epic of my own. In March 2022, my running partner Mike and I decided to run the inaugural Coast Guard Half Marathon/Marathon in Elizabeth City, North Carolina. Mike, a former Coastie, was gung-ho about tackling the Coast Guard's first marathon race, and despite persistent knee pain, I thought it would be a great idea to do the *Semper Paratus* Challenge, which involved running a 5K on Friday night and the half marathon the following morning.

When the 5K started on Friday night, the air felt like the Arctic. A delay of over thirty minutes had everyone shivering uncontrollably, to the point where we could have powered a small generator. The cold triggered some serious questioning of life choices. But eventually, the race began. The plan was to take it easy, knowing the half marathon loomed the next day. But as the finish line approached, a woman in a puffer jacket zipped past. In that moment, something snapped. There was no way a person in a designer coat would beat me. No way. So, I kicked it into high gear, pushing the pace far more than necessary. Who knew a puffer jacket could be so motivational? Chasing her down became my mission. It was a small, silly moment, but it reignited that fire in me, reminding me that running was about pushing limits and proving something to myself.

The next day, Mike and I lined up in the starting corral, ready to tackle the course. The plan was to run together for the first seven miles, easing him into the race. After that, Mike would go solo as the half marathon course split from the full. We kicked off with warmer temperatures than the night before, and it didn't take long to realize I'd overdressed (again). The outfit was perfect for a cozy morning drinking tea, but not so much for a run.

By mile seven, the sun decided to join the party, cranking up the heat and humidity to full "sauna mode."

"Okay, see you at the finish! Good Luck!" I called to Mike as we split.

That's when my knee had other ideas. It buckled, causing me to trip and stumble like a toddler taking their first steps. I mentally kicked myself for pushing too hard the night before to outrun the puffer-jacket lady. My brain screamed, "Keep going!" while my knee shot back with a firm, "Not a chance!"

I've never not finished a race, and it wasn't going to happen today. Mentally and physically gritting my teeth, I switched to a walk/run strategy. It was a long, slow, hot slog of a run. Some of our Wilmington friends near the finish line were cheering like they were at a rock concert. Fueled by their enthusiasm, I made myself run the last stretch and crossed the finish line with a smile in 2:15. Even though I had run a lot of half marathons by this point, 13.1 miles still felt like a lot of miles. It was never "just a half." That distance always reminded me that while running can seem like a simple, straightforward activity, it's not always easy. There were times when my body wasn't cooperating, and that's when relying on the heart kept me moving forward. Running, especially over long distances, often calls for more than just physical strength it demands mental and emotional endurance, too.

Mike finished the full marathon and I cheered him on during the last few miles. It was an exciting day, running in the first-ever USCG race, and the swag was a nice bonus! We drove back to Wilmington, both of us content to have finished, trading stories and reflecting on the day. I knew I'd have to face the music and deal with the reality of my right knee, but that wasn't happening today.

I took the following week off to rest, but the comment from one of the orthopedic doctors began to burrow into my mind like a stubborn splinter. I had brushed it off at the time, but now, it lingered. *Swimming*. Of course, swimming is every orthopedic doctor's go-to suggestion for a runner. "Why don't you try swimming instead of running? Much less pounding on the joints. Much less strain on the body." What they didn't say or maybe didn't realize was that swimming didn't come easy. It wasn't just about jumping in the pool and gliding effortlessly through the water. Swimming required technique, endurance, and a whole new kind of strength. It demanded a different kind of effort, one that felt foreign after years of pounding the pavement. Still, the idea of swimming continued to gnaw at me. Perhaps it was time to give it a try.

Like most people, I could swim. I had splashed around at the beach and floated in pools, but I wasn't what you'd call a *swimmer*. You know, those people who glide through the water like dolphins, effortlessly churning out lap after lap for an hour without ever tiring, coughing, choking, or looking like they were drowning. They do flip turns with the grace of sea otters, making it look so easy and natural.

My friend Sheryl had taken up swimming and triathlons despite her deep-seated fear of water. She learned to swim from scratch as an adult, which I found incredibly inspiring. If she could conquer her fear of the water, surely, I could tackle a few laps. Sheryl encouraged me to join a group swim with the Cape Fear Triathlon Club at the University of North Carolina, Wilmington (UNCW) pool. It felt like the perfect opportunity to dive in, literally and figuratively, and see if I could make swimming work for me.

When I first started swimming, I wasn't expecting it to be a life-changing event, but it was definitely a turning point, much like that groggy morning on the hotel treadmill in Tampa hungover, sweating, and questioning my choices only to end up becoming a runner because of it. A cold, frigid winter day would be my first ever swim workout because why not start swimming on the coldest day of the year? I'd never swum laps before and felt completely clueless, yet there I was at a triathlon club practice. Yes, those present at the practice were "real" triathletes who did IRONMANs on the regular and used a 600-yard swim as a warmup. Talk about feeling like an imposter.

Not to be deterred, using borrowed goggles and a cap from Sheryl, Coaches Trent and Kitty put me in the "slow end" of the pool where I could flail around without interrupting the "real swimmers." After swimming twenty-five yards to the other end and nearly having a heart attack, I then swam back with no sense of form or breath control. I became really good at inhaling water, choking, and appearing to be in distress to the point other swimmers often asked if I was okay.

Swimming felt like trying to run through thick mud each stroke required more effort than it seemed like it should. It wasn't just a change of pace; it was a whole new battlefield. My muscles screamed in ways they never had before, and every breath felt like I had to earn it. The water, which was supposed to be a relief from impact, became its own kind of challenge, an invisible weight that slowed me down, stretched my limits, and left me gasping for air. It wasn't the easy alternative I'd hoped for; it was a different kind of hard.

Trent took pity on me and handed me fins and a kickboard and suggested practicing breathing to the side. Let's just say my initial attempts were less synchronized swimmer and more drowning cat. Forty-five minutes later, exhausted but actually feeling good, I thought, *There might be something to this swimming thing.*

Next thing I knew, a T-shirt and a hat were in hand, officially marking membership in the Cape Fear Triathlon Club.

Somehow, Trent had roped me in without me realizing it. Despite feeling like an imposter among seasoned triathletes, the group was incredibly welcoming and encouraging. Most of them turned out to be former runners dealing with knee issues, which immediately made the situation feel more relatable.

The best part of swimming was it increased the heart rate without aggravating the knees. After each session, there was no soreness, no limping, or need for Ibuprofen. It felt like a revelation. Swim practices continued, and gradually, my efficiency of strokes improved. Stopping to catch my breath at the end of the pool was still necessary, but at least it wasn't the panicked, gasping-for-air feeling of a horror movie scene. Small victories, but they counted.

The results of the hard work quickly became evident. Twice a week, the pool transformed into a place for focus dedicated to drills and targeted workouts that built speed and endurance. What began as a necessary cross-training activity quickly turned into a form of physical therapy, easing knee pain while boosting overall fitness. With every session, progress became more apparent: swimming wasn't just helping it was truly making a difference.

Once the weather and water warmed up, the Tri Club moved outdoors, swimming in the channel at Wrightsville Beach. Banks Channel, a narrow waterway winding through the barrier island, became a playground for jet skis, small boats, kayakers, paddleboarders, and swimmers.

Every Sunday, the Tri Club gathered for an "adventure swim" led by Coach Trent. My first open-water swim with the group was a point-to-point swim. We swam with the current in one direction to the endpoint, then hitched a ride back in someone's truck. Saying I was nervous doesn't quite capture it. I was terrified. I had borrowed a swim buoy, an inflatable flotation device strapped to my waist for visibility to boaters (and sharks). Making things even harder, I had worn my husband's swim shirt, which was way too big for me and created so much drag that I might as well have been towing an anchor. As a beginner swimmer, I had stepped way outside my comfort zone, scared stiff but trying to mask it with a semblance of calm.

Thankfully, a few paddleboarders stayed close, keeping an eye on boat traffic and offering much-needed moral support. Coach Trent assured me he'd stay by my side since my pace was slower than the others'. I started the swim hyperventilating, stopping every few strokes just to catch my breath. Saltwater splashed into my mouth with every stroke, gagging me. Panic set in fast. My brain screamed at me to get out of the water, but Trent kept his cool, coaching me to take deep breaths and relax. I pushed forward a few strokes, then another frantic pause to catch my breath, my heart pounding like I was being chased by a shark. Time blurred, but slowly, the panic subsided. My breathing steadied, and while I wasn't exactly gliding like a graceful swan, I found a rhythm. The farther I swam, the more the fear receded, and bit by bit, the struggle eased.

Trent kept checking in, asking if I wanted to get out, but stubbornly, the answer was always no. Determination kicked in. I was going to swim the entire distance, just like the rest of the group. It took me far longer than everyone else, and I probably cut into Trent's brunch plans, but I pushed through and swam the full two miles in open water. The group finished well ahead of me, but when I finally reached the endpoint, they greeted me with high fives and cheers. I had swallowed a gallon of saltwater and was so exhausted I wasn't sure I'd ever lift my arms again, but the feeling of pride was powerful. I'd stuck it out and conquered my fear.

We all piled into the back of a pickup truck like kids from the '70s, talking and laughing about how fun the swim had been.

A grin spread across my face, wide and uncontainable. I'd been terrified when we started, but somehow I'd pushed through the fear and actually done it. In hindsight, swimming two miles in open water for my first swim probably wasn't the smartest decision. Talk about ambitious. Looking back, it seemed a little wild, crazy even but what's life without a little adventure? This moment proved that the best experiences often come from stepping out of your comfort zone, no matter how daunting it feels at first. And I didn't get eaten by a shark. But rule number one of Tri Club: don't talk about sharks.

As with running, once I started swimming outside, the experience transformed into something entirely different. The Tri Club met early in the mornings to swim before work. We'd be in the ocean working on our strokes, and as we turned to breathe, we'd catch glimpses of the sunrise and the breathtaking hues unfolding above us. It hit me how much of a privilege it was to live near the ocean, able to experience a sunrise swim while many others were stuck commuting, scrolling through Facebook, or watching the news. Instead, we felt like mermaids, gliding through the water, embraced by the beauty of the world waking up around us. There was a downside, though: the ocean creatures jellyfish, to be specific. As summer progressed, their presence increased, and the likelihood of getting stung did too. A jellyfish sting was no picnic, with itching lasting sometimes for weeks. And if that wasn't enough, there were the jellyfish larvae, known as sea lice, which could sneak inside your bathing suit or rash guard, stinging in places you didn't even know existed. It was like mosquito bites multiplied by three; itchy, rash, and burning for at least two weeks. Despite this hazard, I became a regular at the weekly outdoor swims and bike rides with the Tri Club.

Competing in a triathlon had been on my bucket list for years, but the swim component felt like a scary, unscalable wall. Now that the wall no longer existed, it was time to check triathlon off the list. I signed up for our local premier triathlon race, The Wrightsville Beach Sprint Triathlon.

Triathlons came in four distinct distances: the Sprint, which typically includes a 750-meter swim (though it can vary), a roughly twelve-mile bike ride, and a 5K run. Then there was the International Distance, a bit longer, with a 10K run. The Half IRONMAN features a one-mile swim, a fifty-six-mile bike ride, and a half marathon. For the ultimate challenge, the Full IRONMAN included a 1.2-mile swim, a 112-mile bike ride, and a full marathon. Our local Sprint Triathlon was slightly longer than the typical swim, thanks to the current and buoyancy of the saltwater, which gave swimmers an added advantage. It was the perfect introduction to triathlon for someone just dipping a toe into the sport. And I was ready.

Over the summer, swimming became second nature, and the nerves around the swim faded. But a new fear emerged the bike. The course included a local drawbridge, and the thought of crashing there haunted me. I could already picture the drama a "roadside attraction" moment I desperately wanted to avoid. But as the weeks passed, swimming, biking, and the occasional run created a fierce determination to conquer this triathlon.

I took matters into my own hands, Googling everything about transitions and watching YouTube videos to learn how to move efficiently between each discipline. There was a lot of gear involved, and I knew I needed to be prepared. A $150 road bike I found on Facebook Marketplace gave me the feeling of actually being a triathlete, not just a "wannabe" riding a beach cruiser. With the race at the end of September fast approaching, I genuinely felt prepared.

The day before the race, I rolled my bike into the transition area at Wrightsville Beach Park and joined the others, listening to Tom, the race director, give instructions. I walked through the bike transition area, mentally mapping out where to go after the swim and where to move for the run portion.

Triathlons involve a lot of "stuff" shoes, socks, helmet, gloves, sunglasses, towel, water, and fuel, as well as two race bibs one for the bike and one for the run along with markings on my arm and an ankle bracelet for the swim. The anxiety of forgetting something essential loomed over me. I mentally rehearsed everything: taking off the swim cap and goggles, stripping off the rash guard, toweling off, and then putting on socks, shoes, shirt, helmet, gloves, and sunglasses. Meanwhile, the pros made transitions look like a perfectly choreographed dance, zipping through the motions in just one to two minutes while I was stuck in a whirlwind of mental gymnastics. Overwhelmed but also more determined than ever, the race was just one day away, and no matter what, I was going to do this.

The next day, we gathered at dawn at Wrightsville Beach Park, the crisp air filled with excitement. The Tri Club was in full swing, snapping photos and exchanging words of encouragement. As we walked toward the swim start at the Blockade Runner Hotel, a sense of familiarity washed over me. I had swum here all summer and knew the course. Colored caps marked by age and gender made it easy to spot fellow competitors, creating what felt like a triathlon fashion show. My best running friend, Dee, was there, camera in hand, capturing every moment like a proud parent at graduation. I was a bundle of nerves, constantly checking my gear and double-checking my checklist to make sure nothing was forgotten.

Once in the water for a warm-up, the temperature felt perfect not too cold, just refreshing. But the ever-present thought of jellyfish lingered in the back of my mind. Please, no stings today! I hoped to avoid adding "sting victim" to my list of triathlon experiences. When my age group was called over the loudspeaker, Sheryl and I lined up, side by side, treading water, both of us doing our best to look calm and collected. Having her there, a familiar face in the sea of competitors, felt like a life vest for my nerves. The starting gun fired a loud crack and we were off and swimming, crossing Banks Channel, and heading toward Motts Channel. Large buoys bobbed in the water, their bright colors acting as friendly giants, guiding us through the course. The water was smooth, the sky still holding onto the soft shades of early morning light, and for a moment, everything seemed to fall into place. There was no turning back now it was time to swim.

I settled into a rhythm, the water smoothing out beneath me, a calmness coming over me. The steady stroke of my arms, the sound of my breath, and the occasional splash from other swimmers around me created a surprisingly peaceful environment. A few jellyfish drifted by thankfully, just out of reach but the sting of their potential presence didn't faze me. I was in my element, moving forward and feeling strong.

After about twenty-seven minutes of swimming, the ladder at Seapath Towers came into view. I had lost sight of Sheryl along the way, but as I hauled myself out of the water, she was there just ahead of me, climbing the ladder with determination. It felt good to be right there, close behind, sharing the same challenge. I scrambled up and out of the water like a triumphant dolphin breaking the surface. My legs, though a bit wobbly, powered through the transition area as I took off running across the parking lot barefooted, past the cheering spectators. The sound of my name being shouted by friends brought a surge of energy, and a grin spread across my face that I couldn't wipe away. This was it. I had crossed the first hurdle, and now it was time to transition.

As I ran across the wet grass toward the bike transition, I struggled with what felt like an Olympic event: putting socks on my wet feet. It was a slow-motion battle, each sock a challenge, as the clock ticked in my mind. Eventually, I wrestled them on, pulled on my shirt, managed one glove, and then the helmet and sunglasses. By the time I finished, I looked like a fashion statement gone wrong part athlete, part confused tourist.

Steering my bike with one hand, I attempted to run through the transition area, channeling my inner pro. The bike wobbled like a toddler learning to ride, veering unpredictably from side to side. *Why don't they teach this in YouTube videos?* I thought, trying to stabilize the bike while maintaining some semblance of grace. There's a reason the pros make it look easy they've mastered these transitions. For the rest of us, it's a work in progress. The moment my tires hit the smooth concrete, I swung my leg over the bike and started pedaling. The Wrightsville Beach bridge rose into view just minutes ahead. Heart pounding, I summoned every ounce of courage, taking the bridge at a cautious pace. When I crested the top and descended safely on the other side, the tension in my body eased. No crash, no mishap just me and the open road.

The bike course unfolded in a stretch of smooth roads and gentle turns, the sun warming the horizon. The fear of crashing or losing control melted away as soon as I found my rhythm. It felt freeing, like those days back home when I'd ride my old ten-speed up and down the hills, the wind rushing past me. I was a kid again, the world open and full of possibility. It was the kind of joy that reminded me why I loved being active in the first place: freedom, flow, and a little bit of adventure.

The wind felt incredible against my face, and I was never cold. Sipping my electrolytes, I swallowed a gel, a quiet pride settling in as I pushed through. The course stretched about thirteen miles, and as I neared the final leg back over the bridge toward Wrightsville Beach, I spotted my BRFs cheering from the side, their voices rising over the wind, calling my name. I smiled and waved back. In that moment, it all clicked. The miles melted away, and the support of my friends made everything even sweeter.

Crossing back over the bridge, I entered the transition area again. This time, I needed to rack my bike and wrestle with my knee sleeves, which I wore for support on my runs. Stretching them over my sweaty calves was a workout in itself. My hands were slick with sweat, and my arms felt like they were made of lead as I struggled to get the knee sleeves on. After what seemed like an eternity, I managed to get everything situated and took off running only to stumble, my legs like jelly. I staggered forward, completely out of sync. Around me, people echoed my struggles: "I can't run," one said. I could only nod in agreement, hobbling alongside them. But then, one woman laughed and said, "But you are running!" We both giggled at the absurdity of it all, our legs betraying us as we tried to find some semblance of control. A fleeting thought occurred to me: you should probably train to run after riding the bike if you want to actually run after riding a bike. Oops!

After the first mile, my legs began to wake up and find a rhythm, shaking off the stiffness from the bike ride. It had been a while since I'd raced, and I wasn't sure what to expect. But the pace started to pick up, and I passed a few runners, then a few more. The route was familiar, and with every step, I knew exactly when to push harder as the final stretch loomed ahead, the finish line in the distance. My legs were no longer protesting.

The finish line chute stretched out in front of me, lined with friends and familiar faces, all cheering and shouting my name. The energy was electric, infectious, and everything I needed to fuel those final steps. As I crossed the finish line of my first hometown triathlon, a sense of accomplishment flooded me this was a huge personal victory. My legs were tired, and my body was spent, but the feeling of triumph was undeniable. I had done it. And then, fueled by the euphoria of that moment, I signed up for two more triathlons the following year. The variety, the change of pace, the shift from one discipline to another it kept everything fresh. Each race felt new, exciting, and full of possibility. While I didn't follow a strict coach-led plan or an official training program, the summer was filled with swimming and biking, the kind of cross-training that seemed like a new, full-time job. I reduced my running to focus on knee rehab through physical therapy and acupuncture, but the switch-up kept me grounded and mentally sharp during my running hiatus. In a way, the triathlon kept me sane. I found a new tribe in the swimming and biking communities people who motivated me, encouraged me, and reminded me that there was more to fitness than just pounding the pavement.

Still, the Six Star Medal was never far from my thoughts. No matter how much I loved the triathlon world, the dream of conquering the world's most iconic marathons never faded. The seed had been planted six years earlier, during a run with friends, when we'd joked about running through all five boroughs of New York City.

That casual conversation stuck with me. Now, it was time to turn that dream into a reality. I wanted to take on the biggest, most legendary marathon in the world, the New York City Marathon. It was time to lace up my running shoes again. Nothing would hold me back.

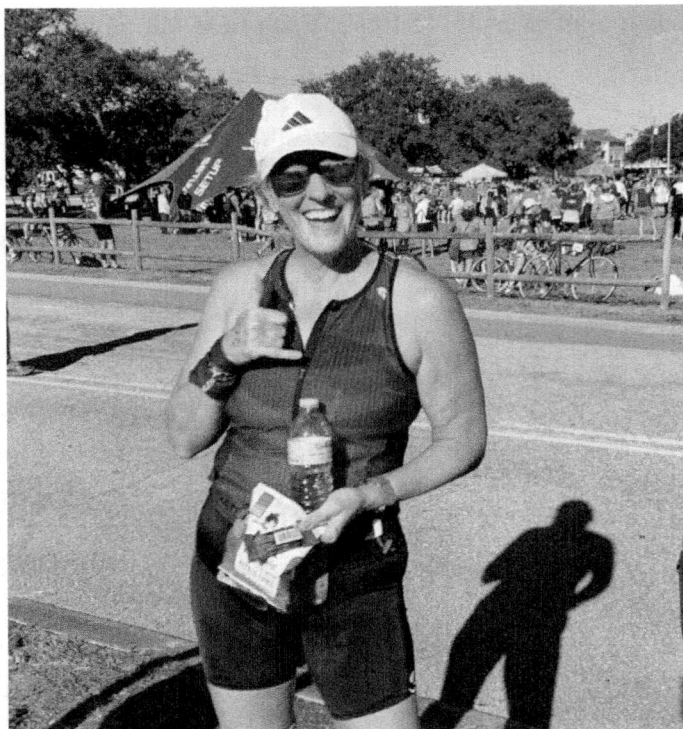

Wrightsville Beach Sprint Triathlon, September 25, 2022

Chapter 14 – Can't Run? Commit to a Marathon

If you Google "suicide disease," trigeminal neuralgia will undoubtedly top the results. The name alone hints at the severity of the condition. The pain is so intense that many who are diagnosed with it contemplate suicide rather than continue enduring the agony. It's a condition that feels almost too cruel to be real: a constant, unrelenting nerve pain in the face, often described as a jolt or shock of electricity. It is present every day, every hour, every minute. It never lets up.

For Scott, trigeminal neuralgia came as a result of either the radiation or the jaw surgery he underwent. What followed was a reality that no one should have to live with: chronic, excruciating pain that gnawed at his face without mercy. The pain, unpredictable and shocking, could strike at any moment. It was as if his face had become the site of a continuous storm, an electrical current pulsing through his nerves without warning. Pain medications like Oxycodone might dull the intensity for a moment, but they don't touch the sensation itself. The burning, the stabbing, the shock don't erase the reality of constant pain, where the body's own signals betray it. Even on the days when he could zone out, the pain would always find him again, dragging him back into that sharp, unbearable reality.

We met with the Trigeminal Nerve Center at Johns Hopkins, hoping for a breakthrough, but they quickly told Scott they couldn't help him. They explained that patients like him those who had undergone radiation weren't studied as much, leaving him with very few solutions. As if the lack of research wasn't bad enough, the chronic pain landscape was even more bleak. With the opioid epidemic raging, there simply weren't any non-addictive medications designed for chronic-pain patients like Scott. The options were devastatingly limited, leaving us to navigate this cruel reality with few answers.

We knew there'd eventually be research breakthroughs and new treatments but there was no relief for the day-in and day-out grind of chronic pain. Every day felt like a slow erosion, a chink in the body armor we both had to fight through, trying to make it to the next moment without losing our composure. The constant struggle wore him down.

Scott's continuously interrupted sleep by the always-present pain left him exhausted and irritable. He'd wake up tired, dragging through the day, only to find the cycle beginning again the next night. The lack of rest compounded the emotional toll of constant discomfort. Facing pain in the late hours of the night can take us down darker paths than we experience in the light of day.

The vicious cycle of nerve pain never seemed to end. Pain, fatigue, frustration, and more pain feeding into each other. No escape, just the ongoing battle to survive each day, hour, and minute. It was exhausting, the weight of it hung over everything we did. Eating became a major challenge for Scott again; every meal involved difficulty, often resulting in him choking or aspirating. He preferred to eat slowly, in the comfort of home. Some days were worse than others, and the constant struggle made eating meals a grueling experience. Thankfully, the days of the feeding tube were over, but his diet became restricted to foods that he could easily swallow, including mashed potatoes, chicken pot pies, and peanut butter crackers. He ate them constantly, every day, with little variation.

Another issue was talking. Scott couldn't talk for long periods without intense pain. Yet, somehow, everyone always wanted to talk to him. He was like the person who doesn't like cats, but the cat won't leave him alone. Scott's tendency to listen more than talk drew people to him, and it seemed uncanny how easily they gravitated toward him. But it frustrated him because he genuinely wanted to engage and was naturally curious about people. As a result of these difficulties with eating and talking, our social life dwindled. Scott, an introvert, didn't mind as much. But for me, it was a different story. Social outings with anyone other than family were rare. We became more isolated both physically and emotionally while navigating this new reality together.

Scott increasingly became more solitary and unable to physically do the activities he used to, but despite having very different interests and capabilities, we found ways to keep doing things as a couple, like camping, hiking, and walking Bodie. We had coffee dates instead of meals. We walked on the beach instead of going to a brewery. Going out to dinner with friends or to a concert was not a part of our lives anymore. If I asked him to go to some social event, the answer was "no" 99 percent of the time. I had to adjust to going solo and becoming the fifth wheel at parties attended by mostly couples. Frustrated, hurt, and feeling cheated by Scott's situation, my anger grew, and I felt sad on occasions despite going to therapy. But I also knew that we were luckier than a lot of other people. While not ideal, we were in it together and muddling through life.

Despite still battling persistent knee pain after trying every remedy available, I decided to go all in and enter the lottery for the New York City Marathon. It was a bold move, almost as if entering would somehow shift the energy and bring an opportunity. The NYC Marathon, with its legendary status and challenging course, had always been at the top of my list. Running across all five boroughs, conquering its steep bridges, and experiencing the renowned energy of the crowds, it was the kind of race that felt like a dream. But luck didn't fall in my favor. The email arrived, and though it was a long shot, a part of me held out hope there would be an entry waiting, but there wasn't. It was a reminder of how much I still wanted to make this goal a reality, even if the path there wasn't going to be easy. It stung but also fueled my determination.

I quickly reached out to Homes for Our Troops, the charity I had run for in the Chicago Marathon, to see if they would let me run for them again. Their mission of building adaptive homes for veterans would rally my network and the funds would be easy to raise. They accepted my application right away, and just like that, the road to my fifth major marathon would happen in New York City.

After a lengthy call with Coach Jen, we discussed if I could train for a marathon running just three days per week, she assured me it could be done.

"Will I be fit enough to run a marathon with only three days a week running?" I asked.

"With cross-training, proper fueling, and rest days, you can do this," she told me.

Coach Jen's plan, designed specifically to help me train for the marathon without overloading my knee, centered around three days of running each week, a significant reduction from the usual four to six days. I felt the weight of doubt creep in could this marathon plan work with so few runs? But Jen reassured me, reminding me that the cross-training I'd been doing over the past year had built a solid foundation. Paramount to this plan would be recovery. We'd extended the training cycle to give my body time to adjust, ensuring I wouldn't rush back into full marathon training too quickly.

At the start, my runs were short, just a few miles at a time, so I could rebuild my stamina without taxing my knee with no particular pace or time goal. The focus was clear: finish strong enough to keep running after the marathon was over. It wasn't about achieving greatness or running a personal best but, instead, being able to keep running for years to come. Letting go of that old pressure felt like the removal of a heavy weight after so much time spent trying to be "faster" and "better" without understanding what those words meant. Surrendering to the process opened my eyes to a different kind of power, one rooted in patience, consistency, and acceptance. A quiet strength, the kind that didn't demand to be noticed but was felt deep down with each stride. Funny how surrendering to something you're holding on to so tightly actually gives you freedom.

As June rolled in, training began in earnest. Runs started with a mix of walking and easy-paced running nothing intense, just easing my body back into the rhythm of running. These runs were complemented with cross-training in the gym, swimming, and cycling, which kept my fitness up without straining my knee. Speed workouts were out of the question for now; my knee couldn't handle any fast-paced running or hilly routes. Every time I tried, it pushed back, reminding me that my body wasn't ready to go full speed. The frustration was real, especially on days when I watched other runners pushing hard in their workouts. But every setback reminded me of the bigger picture: speed or distance aren't the only ways to measure strength. It's found in persistence, in showing up again and again, even when it feels like progress is slow or barely noticeable. Each time I tied my shoes and hit the pavement, my strength increased, not just physically but mentally. I was learning to be okay with accepting the process for what it was. And in that acceptance, I found a kind of peace that I'd never experienced in all my years of running.

Kelsey, Idaho Barb's niece, pushed me hard in the gym. Together, we lifted Olympic-style weights, flipped tires, and pushed sleds, all designed to build power. Each session left me feeling more solid and more resilient. In August 2022, I committed to a 30-day challenge 100 push-ups, 100 squats, and 100 sit-ups every day. The first few days, it felt like I could barely do anything. But slowly, my core tightened and my strength increased. Inch by inch, I built muscle and endurance, proving that even the smallest efforts add up to something significant.

Then, the brutal reality of summer training hit. *Oh my God*, I thought, *another summer training session*. To escape the scorching North Carolina heat, where the pavement could fry eggs, I sought refuge in the North Carolina mountains, tackling long runs and never-ending hills. My running mates spent many a Sunday morning running up and over the Topsail Island Bridge in Surf City to practice gaining and losing elevation. It became our second home; we could practically offer guided tours. Occasionally, my training crew ventured to Raleigh, taking on the hills at Umstead State Park, logging 1,900 to 2,000 feet of elevation gain on each long run. Every step was grueling, but my running buddies stayed right there, giving encouragement, keeping me upright, and offering to pause my Garmin when I threatened to collapse.

Clinging to the run/walk method like a lifeline, the brief walking breaks eased the pounding on my knees. The heat, suffocating and unyielding, made each run feel like an endurance test. My body demanded fuel, so I slurped down electrolytes, gulped protein shakes, and snacked as if preparing for a journey through the desert. When my muscles screamed for rest, I listened, giving myself permission to slow down and recover.

The training felt awful, by far the hardest yet. Every mile seemed like a battle. At times, each step was cursed, with vows to never again train in North Carolina's oppressive summer heat. Do you know the magic of marathon training? It sneaks up on you. The improvements go unnoticed at first. You don't see how much stronger you get with every session, even when the pace isn't setting records. Resilience quietly builds, one run at a time. Slowly, the body adapts. By mid-August, we started hill repeats and track intervals adding a new layer of challenge. The knees held up but not always without protest. Self-care and rest days overtook most weekends.

To gauge progress, I signed up for the Marine Corps Half Marathon at Camp LeJeune, a race in early September, which in North Carolina is the definition of miserable. The heat blazed, and the humidity wrapped itself around me like a wool coat in a sauna. I knew this would be awful. But a tough race would give me a true measure of where my marathon training stood. My friends Mailyn and Anderson rode up to Jacksonville, North Carolina, with me, and we sat in the car, staring at the pouring rain like spectators at a bad movie.

"Why did we sign up for this?"

"I don't want to get out of the car."

"C'mon, let's get this over with."

Reluctantly, we forced ourselves out of the car and into the deluge, lining up at the start. The rain hammered down, and humidity clung to every inch. We were drenched, and our doubts swirled. *Why am I doing this stupid race? I hate Jacksonville. I hate this weather. This is going to suck.* The national anthem played, the gun fired, and we surged forward like a pack of soggy ducks.

The first five miles passed, the overcast skies and steady rain providing conditions for a relaxed pace. I chatted with Sheryl, who had also decided to punish herself. Nonetheless, we tried to enjoy the moment and convince ourselves the rain felt refreshing rather than draining.

We had a steady rhythm, and the miles seemed to tick off. But by mile seven, things started to shift. A telltale tightness in my lower back flared up, a familiar signal of dehydration. Just as I tried to adjust my stride to shake off the discomfort, the rain stopped, the clouds parted, and the sun suddenly vengeful broke through with a force that felt almost intentional, like it was punishing all of us who had dared to hope for a cooler race. The temperature shot up, and what had been a rainy albeit decent running day turned into a brutal test of willpower. It felt as though we were running through a thick steam bath, each step dragging through sticky air, the weight of it settling on my shoulders and chest. I looked at the runners around me, all of us struggling to push forward. It wasn't just the heat it was the way the humidity clung to every inch of skin, an obstinate presence that wanted to zap any remaining energy. The cramps in my back worsened, and I felt the toll the heat was taking. The pace slowed for everyone. What had been a smooth race just moments before now became a battle. My legs grew heavy, each stride harder than the last. Sweat poured down in rivulets, mixing with the remnants of rainwater still on my face. I wasn't alone in this suffering others around me looked equally miserable, dragging their feet, fighting their bodies to keep moving.

Eventually, the finish line came into view, a distant banner that somehow seemed both too far and too close. The final stretch dragged on, the last half mile tedious and seemingly endless, as if the course had been extended just to prolong the pain. When I crossed at 2:31, the time felt like a defeat. I had expected more from myself after all, I'd put in the work, and I knew I was capable of better. But the heat, the cramps, the dehydration had taken a toll. Once I caught my breath and reminded myself that this race was just a checkpoint, not a finish line, and that this was a test of fitness in the worst conditions, disappointment still lingered, but only briefly. There was more work to do, more miles to run, and the marathon promised to be cooler in November.

By early October, the brutal heat started to ease, and the mornings grew dark again, signaling the arrival of Fall. While the cooler weather was a relief, I found myself facing an unexpected hurdle. My feet had become a disaster zone. Blisters, black toenails, or toenails missing altogether. Honestly, my feet looked like something straight out of a horror movie, and every time I removed my shoes, I half expected a scream track to play in the background.

As any runner knows, shoe manufacturers like to switch up their designs just when you have found the perfect running shoe. A cruel trick, the kind that keeps us in a perpetual state of foot-related panic. The once-comfortable fit turned into a daily source of misery. Feeling desperate, I texted Michelle, the owner of Fleet Feet, a true shoe-fitting savant.

"Please help! My feet are a disaster!"

If there's anyone who knows the magic behind the perfect fit, it's Michelle. She didn't disappoint. With her expertise, we switched brands, added custom inserts, and after a few painful adjustments, my feet stopped feeling like they were under siege. I could actually run without wincing with every step I took. It was like walking on clouds, a feeling I hadn't experienced in weeks. To speed up the recovery, soaking in Epsom salts became a daily treatment. Slowly but surely, the blisters healed, and my toenails well, they grew back in their own way and at their own pace.

At the beginning of October, I completed my first of two, twenty-mile-long runs. The pace wasn't fast, but the miles were in the bank, as was the feeling of satisfaction of having tackled a significant distance. A small victory for my beleaguered feet. Meanwhile, Tracy, one of my closest running buddies, steadily built her mileage alongside mine. She'd never run more than thirteen miles, so each week, we ventured into new mileage territory together. Watching her cross milestones that I'd once fought through myself was pure joy. It's one of the most rewarding experiences as a runner seeing a friend push past their limits and grow stronger, especially when you've walked that same difficult road. Our long runs became more than just training; they were filled with conversations about life, goals, kids, dating, football, and everything in between. In those moments, when the miles seemed to tick by, we knew the magic of running lies in the journey itself. By mid-October, Tracy and I did another twenty-mile long run, and at mile seventeen, something clicked.

"Let's keep going and do twenty-two miles. My legs feel strong." Always willing to test her limits, she agreed.

"Okay, I've never gone that far, but let's go for it."

Tracy hung in there and by the end, we were both celebrating our endurance and growth as runners. I couldn't have been prouder of her. That post-run feeling was electric, buzzing with endorphins. After coming home, I cranked up some rock music and danced around the house while Scott watched and laughed at my solo dance party. After running twenty-two miles, I'd taken complete leave of my senses but didn't care. My last long run before tapering? Classic. My log read, "Knees hurt really bad, but I had a good run." And that summed up my entire training cycle: the knees may have protested, but we got it done, one step at a time.

I met my BRFs on the Thursday before race day for one last easy run, followed by coffee. We chatted about all those tough hill runs in Raleigh and back and forth over the Topsail Island Bridge, laughing at the shared memories of sweaty and grueling miles. They wished me well for the marathon, and I took a moment to thank them for their unwavering support. From barely running a few miles due to knee pain to swimming, surviving another brutal summer training cycle, and completing my first triathlon now here I was, preparing for my fifth World Marathon Major, in the biggest marathon in the world. Who would have thought? Step by step, little by little, each day had added up to something much bigger.

The fundraising for my race had gone better than expected. Thanks to the incredible mission of Homes for Our Troops, I easily met my goal through crowdfunding with friends, family, and colleagues. My CEO, VPs, and coworkers were huge supporters. Their generosity left me feeling deeply grateful. Supporting veterans and helping them live fuller, more independent lives felt incredibly meaningful. Later, I learned that the donations from this race helped Homes for Our Troops build a house for a veteran in Durham, North Carolina. To know that my effort, however small, contributed to improving a veteran's life in my home state was a profound reminder of the impact we can all have, even through the toughest challenges.

Chapter 15 – New York City Marathon 2022

My heart started racing and panic set in. *What if I don't get to New York in time to get my race packet?* It was Friday, November 4, 2022, and flights to New York were delayed for hours, many rerouted due to dense fog at all three of the city's airports. My phone buzzed nonstop with horror stories of friends rerouted to Rochester, layovers lasting over four hours, and fears they might never get there.

My flight was set to leave on Saturday, November 5. Danielle, my friend and neighbor, had agreed to join me as my trusty logistical and post-race helper. Months earlier, I'd booked a room at the Hilton Hotel in midtown Manhattan, perfectly situated near the finish line. With multiple visits to New York under my belt, the airport, hotel, and surroundings felt like second nature. I'd deliberately scheduled my flight for the day before the race, while many of my local friends had flown out on Friday. As text messages detailing my friends' travel woes multiplied, the anxiety about my own flight crept in. Picking up my race packet was non-negotiable. With no bib pickup on race day, I had to get there on time. I mentally scolded myself for not booking an earlier flight and even toyed with the idea of driving to New York.

"Maybe we should just drive to New York," I suggested, half joking. "If we leave tonight, we'll get there by Saturday morning." Scott and Danielle stared at me, wide-eyed.

"You're not serious? We will get there, it's a direct flight. We are leaving first thing in the morning," Danielle reassured me.

Thankfully, Danielle and Scott talked me off the ledge. Our flight left on time, and we breezed through LaGuardia without a single hiccup.

We taxied through Manhattan to our hotel, taking in the New York scenery, the skyscrapers, the people, the street vendors; the city pulsated with energy. As it turned out, many runners were staying at our hotel and were proudly wearing finisher jackets from Boston and other World Major races. After we dropped off our bags, we hopped into an Uber and headed to the expo at the Jacob Javits Center. This expo was massive and over-the-top. There were legendary runners speaking on various topics, loads of vendors, and an abundance of marathon gear. We browsed through all the merchandise, emerging victorious with tank tops, T-shirts, and, of course, the coveted marathon finisher jacket. We found my name on the wall of starters and snapped a few photos.

Afterward, keeping with my carb-loading plan, we found a Chinese restaurant where I loaded up on rice and protein like a marathon-fueling machine. We ventured to the Fleet Feet store near the finish line and picked up even more gear. Knowing that I needed to save my legs (and knees), we headed back to the Hilton to rest, eat, and hydrate for the remainder of the evening. No more rookie mistakes.

The New York City Marathon, being the largest in the world, draws over fifty thousand runners. With that size came logistical nightmares. The race wove through all five boroughs of New York, starting in Staten Island, followed by Brooklyn, Queens, the Bronx, and ending in Central Park, Manhattan. It's a famed course with unforgettable crowds and jaw-dropping scenery, but to pull it off, organizers had to navigate some serious challenges, including closing roads and bridges before dawn to ensure runners' safety. This meant getting tens of thousands of athletes onto a small island before the major thoroughfares shut down. And all this in a city of eight million people. Runners have two options to get to the start: ferry or bus. Buses leave from various hotels in Manhattan around 6:00 a.m., which meant you waited on

Staten Island in the athlete village for four or five hours before your corral was called to the start line. I opted for the Staten Island Ferry from Lower Manhattan to catch a glimpse of the Statue of Liberty and take in the spectacular views of New York City's skyline on the way to the start. Who wouldn't want a little pre-race sightseeing?

The morning began at 5:00 a.m. with tackling the twelve-mile journey to the start. I met several folks from the NYC Marathon Facebook group at the Times Square subway station at 6:00 a.m. Having a group made me feel more at ease, especially since one woman had run New York several times and knew the ropes. Still, we didn't anticipate just how packed the subway would be. This was only a year after COVID. Being in such a massive crowd felt a bit unnerving.

We piled into the subway, standing room only, shoulder to shoulder. Our group stood together and chatted excitedly for the day to come. Once we got off the subway, we entered the ferry terminal, which was jam-packed with runners. We waited an hour for a ferry with people pushing and shoving to get to the front of the line. By now, I regretted my decision. The 6:00 am buses had already dropped off runners who were resting and hydrating. But it was too late to change course, so we waited, packed in like cattle. At one point, we actually had to hold hands to stay together.

Once we boarded the ferry, we found some breathing room. I started snapping photos of the skyline and Lady Liberty. It was a beautiful scenic ride. The temperatures were warm, too, hovering in the upper 60s. This was definitely not going to be a typical chilly November race. Lucky me, it was going to be hot, humid, and tough.

I thought about all my friends running New York who had big goals. From my past experiences, I knew that when the weather doesn't cooperate, it's time to adjust expectations. I didn't have a specific time goal, just the aim to finish. With my knees acting up and the warm temperatures, I knew I needed to stick to my run/walk plan and keep my pace easy while hydrating. If I wanted to finish this race and snag my fifth star, I had to manage the heat, the humidity, the hills, and, most importantly, my mind. Staying mentally tough was imperative if I wanted to cross the finish line.

As soon as we disembarked the ferry, the warmth hit me, and like a snake molting its skin, I shed my throwaway clothes. At the bus loading area, our group joined the wall of people, literally thousands crammed together, jockeying for a spot on a bus that would take us to the athlete village and start area.

With this being the first New York City Marathon post-COVID, I wondered if they'd forgotten how to organize such a massive event. With the crowd swelling and tempers flaring, it was mayhem. People were angry, insults were flying, and those classic New Jersey and New York accents were out in full force, yelling, cursing, and demanding that the volunteers let them on the buses. I won't lie, it was scary.

After two hours of waiting, (yes, you read that right) I finally got on a bus. I was sad I lost my group in the process but stood waving from my seat like a contestant on a game show, wishing them luck as I rode away. I made it to the athlete village area at 10:30 a.m. It took me over four hours to cover just twelve miles. When runners ask if they should take the bus or ferry, I always say "Take the bus." The Staten Island Ferry is free, and you can see the Statue of Liberty another day.

Fortunately, being a slower runner meant I had a later start time at 11:30 a.m. After all that shuffling around, getting to the subway station at 6:00 a.m., riding to Lower Manhattan, standing in line for the ferry, and then enduring another two-hour line for the bus, I had already clocked over ten thousand steps before the race even began.

I grabbed a cup of tea, a banana, and a bagel, then plopped down to relax after the harrowing morning. I was still shaking from the stress, so I took some deep breaths while watching everyone else stretch, fuel up, and mill around. Thankfully, the blazing sun gave way to clouds, and it started to drizzle a bit. Good news for us later waves. The earlier runners had faced the full brunt of the sun's wrath.

Soon, my corral was called, and we lined up to head to the Verrazano Bridge. The excitement was palpable; everyone was whooping and yelling. As we stepped onto the bridge, the organizers cranked up "New York, New York" by Frank Sinatra. Everyone started singing and laughing, creating an electric and infectious vibe. There was really nothing like the start of a marathon. The energy, the excitement. It's indescribable. I thought about all the work that had brought me here. The rehab for my knees, those grueling gym workouts, the training runs in the sweltering heat all summer, and the relentless hill training in the mountains, in Raleigh, and over the Topsail Bridge. I could still feel the pain in my knees, but now, standing on this amazing bridge in New York, and getting ready to run the biggest race in the world, I couldn't wait to get going. I also thought of Scott back home, tracking me on his phone and waiting for the phone call when I finished.

Once the gun went off, we started our watches and began running. The beginning featured a bit of an incline to get up and over the bridge, but once we covered the bridge, we were officially in Brooklyn for the first half of the race. The unique neighborhoods, quirky architecture, vibrant flowers, and leftover Halloween decorations were all on display, but what made Brooklyn truly special were the crowds. They came out in full force to cheer us on.

And when I say full force, I mean they were packed in so tightly that only three or four runners could squeeze through at a time. You had no choice but to slow down as you navigated through the sea of spectators yelling, cheering, and screaming. It was amazing. Music blasted from every corner, including rock bands, DJs, school bands, boom boxes, you name it. There was no way to describe the sheer energy from the masses surrounding us, all pumped up and cheering their hearts out. These folks had been out there all morning, and they were still going wild for us. Although not everyone thrives in this kind of chaotic environment during a race, I absolutely loved it and fully embraced the spirited mood of the spectators and participants. I passed by some outrageous costumes, including men in tutus and one guy casually munching on a pizza while running. There were moments when it felt like a game of dodgeball, with people crossing the course and nearly colliding everywhere. The potholes and rough road conditions kept me on my toes, but that was all part of the wonderful pandemonium. I focused on hydrating and stuck to my run/walk plan. The course was relatively flat at first, but I knew hills lurked just around the corner.

At the halfway mark, I entered Queens and was greeted by the massive Queensboro Bridge. This uphill monster seemed to go on for miles. I put my head down and thought, *okay, here we go, the hills begin now*. Many runners around me started to walk, but I stayed the course and kept forging ahead. I felt good and maintained a steady pace. The views from the top of the bridge were breathtaking. The Manhattan skyline loomed in front of me, and it was eerily quiet since there were no spectators on the bridge. I savored that brief moment of silence, but it didn't last long. Soon, the roar of the crowds waiting just ahead filled the air. I practically flew down the glorious hill off the bridge and turned onto First Avenue, which was massive and lined with onlookers four to six people deep. It was a sneaky uphill, so I had to stay sharp. As I ran through the Bronx, the music was loud enough that I could feel the beat pulsing in my chest. I had no idea what song was playing, but it was absolutely exhilarating!

Before I knew it, I was in Harlem and then Manhattan. By mile twenty, nature called, and I desperately needed to find a porta-john. I had hydrated so well that I unexpectedly found myself needing to pee. Getting back into my rhythm after that stop was tough, and it took me a solid half mile to find my groove again, but I was still in the race.

The course through Central Park was stunning, especially in early November when the trees burst with autumn colors. But those hills late in the race? A brutal test for both mind and body. Fifth Avenue, miles twenty-three to twenty-four snuck up on me with their long, brutal inclines. Thankfully, the beautiful trees and signature high rise buildings provided a welcome distraction. As I climbed Fifth Avenue, I spotted Debra, another Strava friend, in the crowd. Strava had connected us years earlier during the pandemic, but we'd never met in person. Seeing her smiling face gave me such a boost. We managed a quick hug before I was off and running again. I pushed deeper into Central Park, walking a bit more but still keeping the momentum. The cheers from the crowd rang in my ears, offering the classic "almost there" the phrase every marathon runner loves to hate.

The final stretch on 59th Street felt uphill, too. I started cussing in my mind. *How many effing hills are there?* When I turned back into the park, it was like a cruel joke: another incline. I was exhausted, but still the massive crowds yelled words of encouragement. I couldn't help but think of professional American runner Shalane Flanagan in this exact spot, raising her fist and shouting, "F*ck Yeah!" when she won the New York City Marathon in 2017. Here I was, finishing the biggest marathon in the world and earning my fifth star. My body was screaming to stop but I saw the eight-hundred-meter sign, then four hundred meters, then two hundred meters, and finally the finish line. I crossed that line feeling relieved and happy, clocking in at 5:10:53. Not my fastest, but certainly not my slowest, either. And honestly? I didn't have a single qualm about finishing over five hours. I had maintained a steady pace throughout and discovered later that my splits were consistent.

Remarkably, I crossed the finish line with the Tommy Puzey, better known as "Rivs". Rivs was an ultra-marathoner, a physical therapist, an endurance coach, and a devoted father of two young girls, all while being a beacon in the Flagstaff, Arizona, running community. He had faced an undiagnosed respiratory illness, later revealed to be an aggressive cancer that nearly claimed his life. He'd been in a coma, teetering on the edge of death, but through sheer will and resilience, he emerged from that darkness to reclaim his life and his passion for running. I followed his extraordinary journey on Instagram, and just weeks before, I'd listened to endurance athlete and podcaster Rich Roll interview Rivs. It brought me to tears. As we moved through the finish line chute, I couldn't contain my excitement at meeting him in person.

"I heard you on the Rich Roll podcast and you made me cry," I told him. He smiled through his thick beard.

"It made me cry, too," he said.

I shared a glimpse of my own struggles, telling him about Scott's battle with cancer and how Rivs's story had lit a spark in my heart. Rivs was nothing short of radiant, his energy calm yet powerful, a soothing presence amidst the craziness of the finish line area. It was like we were in our own cocoon, having a deep, meaningful conversation. He started to run away to meet his friends, but he turned back, wrapped me in a warm embrace, and said he was thrilled to hear Scott was doing better. "Congratulations on finishing," he added, his words wrapping around me like a comforting blanket. We snapped a quick photo, and in that fleeting moment, it felt as if the universe aligned.

Finishing the race alongside Rivs wasn't just a highlight it was a poignant reminder of the strength of the human spirit. In the heart of the city, amidst the cheers and the sweat, I felt a runner connection that transcended the miles, a celebration of resilience, hope, and the unbreakable bonds we forge along the way. The finish chute in New York was legendary, and for good reason.

After finishing, I embarked on what felt like a trek of epic proportions. We walked, shuffled, and meandered for nearly a mile north to exit Central Park. Just when we thought we were done, we turned around and made the long journey back south to Columbus Circle to the family and friends area. Along the way, volunteers handed out food, drinks, and incredible fleece-lined ponchos. Normally, in the brisk November New York air, this was a brilliant touch, but the warm temperatures made it just another item to lug as we limped along, our bodies aching. My knees were locking up, and as I walked, the emotions started to overwhelm me. By the time I spotted Danielle, I was bawling, tears streaming down my face, a mixture of exhaustion and sheer relief. The finish area was a frenzy of excitement, with runners still on the course and crowds cheering all around us.

"You did it! I'm so proud of you," she said.

"Oh my god, I'm in so much pain," I replied. She had my change of clothes, and I switched out my shoes and put on a dry shirt. After what felt like an eternity, we made it back to the mid-town Hilton. The moment I collapsed onto the bed, I felt as if I'd been hit by a truck. All I wanted was to soak in a hot bath and devour everything in sight. I had been on the go since 6:00 a.m. Now it was 8:00 p.m., and it had been a true marathon of a day.

"I want nachos so bad!" I told Danielle.

Danielle understood my craving but, despite her best efforts, couldn't find a place that served them. Instead, she managed to scrounge up some quesadillas and chips that I happily devoured, plus her leftover sandwich from lunch. We slipped into our pajamas and began to relive the day.

Danielle had spent the day sightseeing and shopping. She then made her way over to the course and found a spot near the finish line about the same time I crossed it, but somehow, we missed each other in the sea of people. The day had been long, but nothing could dampen my elation. I'd just completed my fifth World Major. As I gazed down at the enormous New York City Marathon medal around my neck, a laugh escaped. It was like a trophy for surviving a grueling obstacle course.

The race wasn't just an athletic event it was an epic journey packed with logistical challenges, and huge crowds. This was a day that certainly felt like multiple marathons. But every minute was worth it. The energy from the crowd was infectious, and running through all five boroughs? There's nothing like it. The bridges, the diverse neighborhoods, the stunning fall colors in Central Park it all felt like something out of a dream. Brooklyn? Well, it stole my heart. Forever.

On Monday, Danielle and I spent the day strolling around the city, taking photos with my medal in Times Square, Central Park, Saks Fifth Avenue, and Rockefeller Center. We even bumped into pro-runner and top woman American finisher Aliphine Tuliamuk in the lobby of our hotel. For me, a celebrity sighting! I had seen her win the Olympic trials back in Atlanta right before the pandemic shut the entire world down. Completely star-struck, we shared memories of that day and chatted for a few minutes. I felt like I had met a friend.

After all that excitement, we snagged an Uber to LaGuardia, and I finally indulged in my long-craved nachos and champagne at the airport, my favorite post-race feast. I felt so proud of myself for fueling well, carb-loading like a champ, and running a consistent race. Plus, I had a blast! No GI distress, no frantic runs to the porta-john at mile sixteen, and zero cramping. Most importantly, I felt no disappointment in my finish time and didn't worry about what anyone else might think of my race. I had finally started to get the hang of this marathon thing. I caught my breath, the euphoria of crossing the finish line still coursing in my veins. It was time to pivot and plot the next big adventure. Tokyo.

The Tokyo Marathon is one of the most elusive, notoriously difficult races to get into. The hurdles of gaining entry could be almost as challenging as the race itself. But I wouldn't back down. Thankfully, with a little luck, it didn't take long before I had secured my spot. A trip to Japan turned from a distant dream into an exciting reality.

New York City Marathon, November 6, 2022

With Tommy "Rivs" Puzey at the New York City Marathon
finish line

Chapter 16 – Run as One

A few weeks after the NYC marathon, despite my knees feeling like they were going to break into a million pieces, I laced up my shoes again. I cannot put into words what goes through a runner's mind when they're injured and should stop running other than to say it's complete denial. I'm positive that my non-running friends and family were flummoxed that I continued to run, since they told me repeatedly to look for other hobbies. My running friends wisely said nothing and understood that I would eventually get dealt my dose of reality. Still, even as my body protested, my mind was already fixated on the next challenge: running Tokyo and earning that Six Star Medal.

The Tokyo Marathon, established just seventeen years ago, was the youngest of the World Marathon Majors. It took place on the first Sunday in March and accommodated about thirty-five thousand runners. Securing an entry proved challenging, especially for international participants. Elite athletes could earn a spot through time qualifications. Otherwise, charity runners could gain entry through their charities, though the application process for these entries was complex and proved difficult to navigate due to the language barrier. A general lottery existed, but when three hundred thousand people are competing for roughly thirty thousand available spots, it's not great odds.

During the pandemic, the Tokyo Marathon organizers postponed the 2021 marathon until March 2022 but still called it the 2021 Tokyo Marathon and barred international athletes from racing. They canceled the 2022 marathon and transferred all participants to 2023. Because Japan was slower to reopen and resume normal activities, people had been waiting *for years* to run the race. I watched this play out on the World Marathon Majors Challenge Facebook group page, and I felt bad for the runners who had waited so long for updates from the Tokyo Marathon organizers.

Wisely, I decided that I would make Tokyo my last Six Star race in hopes that the backlog would clear out and the race would return to normal. I also felt that I wanted to experience this once-in-a-lifetime trip to Japan when all thoughts of the pandemic were over and there were no longer any restrictions. I began the research on gaining entrance into the marathon when I discovered that the Tokyo Marathon offered a contest called "Run as One." This competition was an alternative route to the regular "pray for entry" lottery. Each month, runners pay a small registration fee, complete a virtual half marathon, and enter a drawing for a chance to secure a spot in the marathon. If your number was drawn, you earned the opportunity to register for the Tokyo Marathon.

My friend Deb had entered through the Run as One program and won a spot on her first try. She mentioned that a new session would open just a few weeks after I completed New York. The virtual option proved ideal, as it didn't require running for time, it allowed for walking or running, and participants could spread the effort over several days. The most challenging aspect involved using the app correctly to record the time and submit it to the Tokyo Marathon website. This marked the start of what I would soon recognize as the "Japanese way" a system filled with rules and, at times, unnecessarily complicated processes.

I ran with the Wilmington Road Runners Club on a Saturday long run to record my half marathon in Runkeeper and submitted to the Run as One program a few weeks after the New York City Marathon. Once entered, I had to wait approximately two weeks before the drawing would take place. I told everyone I would submit an entry every month for the next year if I had to. Once I posted my time from Runkeeper, I received an email from the marathon organizers assigning me a number. The winning numbers were sent out by the race organizers on a Sunday. I carefully looked at all the numbers and saw my number listed as a winner. I started jumping up and down in my home office. I couldn't believe my luck, and I didn't truly believe it until I got the official email on Monday, December 12, 2022, titled, "You Are the Winner!" Completely ecstatic that I would get my sixth star in Japan, I was also over the moon, thrilled that Scott and I would go to Japan together.

With a 2024 Tokyo Marathon entry secured in December 2022, I had ample time to plan, build strength, and focus on my health. But I also took time to step away from training and enjoy other activities. I considered this essential not just for my body, but for my mind as well. Running, like many sports, demanded mental toughness, and taking a break helped keep me motivated. I completed two more triathlons, went skiing, and even paced my 22nd half marathon. As my friend Brad put it, "Let's ditch all these races and run like third graders at recess." My goal became running simply for fun.

Despite my knees continuing to trouble me, I had already signed up for and planned a trip with friends to run the Big

Sur Marathon Relay in April 2023 in California, a bucket-list event. We registered as a team in the summer of 2022, knowing the race sold out quickly, and for good reason. The Big Sur Marathon claimed the title of the most beautiful race in the U.S., offering something for everyone along one of the most scenic highways in the world. The race began in Big Sur and finished in Carmel, California, on the Pacific Coast Highway. The centerpiece of the race stood at the Bixby Bridge, where a tuxedo-clad concert pianist played a grand piano on the scenic overlook. The organizers actually hauled a Yamaha AvantGrand piano to this remote spot, just for the runners' enjoyment.

Like New York, Big Sur posed a massive logistical challenge that required extensive road closures and rerouted traffic to keep runners safe on the winding mountain passes. We all groaned when we learned that buses picked up relay runners at 3:00 a.m. to ensure they arrived at their designated points along the course. Wake-up call was 1:45 a.m. or thereabouts, which made us laugh since that used to be our "arrive home from a night on the town" time.

My friend Amanda found us an incredible Airbnb in Salinas situated on a working winery. The property charmed us with its beautiful architecture, rows and rows of grape vines, and funny mountain goats for neighbors. The downside was the twenty to thirty minutes travel time from the property to our bus meetup point. We meticulously planned and charted our transportation, a change of clothes, throwaway clothes, snacks, drinks, and the connecting meetup points. By the time we finished, it looked like a logistical masterpiece that could've been used to get a grand piano to the Bixby Bridge.

Race morning, we dragged ourselves out of bed after only a few hours of sleep and drove to the bus depot/school parking lot. With our snacks, clothes, and coffees, we joined the crowd of runners already queued up, everyone waiting for the designated bus that would transport their group to the relay point. It was complete mayhem, but even more so as we were all half asleep. Of course, the bus I boarded had a group of ladies who couldn't stop talking at 3:30 a.m. We arrived at our relay spot about seven miles from the start, where we waited for the race to begin and the sun to rise. I tried to sleep or at least rest, but the incessant talking about absolutely nothing was making my head hurt.

I stepped outside to escape their chatter and met a full-on gale. The wind howled and roared through the mountains. Our bus sat perched alongside a narrow strip of road with the ocean far below making for a tight squeeze once the full marathon and relay runners started arriving. The runners had to run uphill into the wind and had their work cut out for them. One last bathroom break before race time had me pushing through the gusty air to the facilities. As I approached the porta-john, the wind slammed open the door, but thankfully, no one was on the toilet for the whole race to see. I struggled to get the door closed and started laughing at the ridiculousness of the situation. We actually paid to do this.

Cell service remained spotty, but once daylight arrived, we texted photos from our locations. The views stunned us. My friend Robin handled the first eight-mile leg starting in Big Sur before joining me for the seven-mile, second leg. It was so cold and windy; I didn't want to leave the warmth of the bus, even with the chatty Cathies still yakking away. Once I saw Robin, I jumped out and gave her a big hug, and we set off to climb the mountain for two miles to Hurricane Point, then make a long downhill run toward the Bixby Bridge, where the pianist played at the scenic overlook. Robin and I marveled at the views. The scenery, unreal in its beauty, looked like something out of a painting. We took photo after photo as we climbed and climbed the mountain. Somewhere along the way, we started giggling, and by the time we got to the top of the famous Hurricane Point, where the wind was blowing at hurricane strength, we were roaring with laughter.

Our clothes were twisting around our bodies, our sunglasses were being blown off our faces, and our skin rippled from being blown sideways. It was beyond crazy; it was ridiculous and hilarious. I wasn't able to capture many photos at the top since it was pandemonium, but we enjoyed the gorgeous views before we made our way down the mountain.

My knees screamed in protest on the downhill, but the moment we heard the opening chords of *Tiny Dancer* by Elton John drifting through the mountains, I willed myself to forget the pain. As we neared Bixby Bridge, the pianist transitioned seamlessly into the *Chariots of Fire* theme song, and the whole scene was beautiful. The music echoed off the cliffs, swirling through the air, turning the already breathtaking landscape into something surreal and magical. I had full-body chills running down the mountain and hearing that beautiful piano playing. We snapped photos and videos, soaking up the atmosphere. Before we knew it, we were at the next relay point, and our friend Carey was due to take over. We all hugged, high-fived, and sent Carey off to run her portion.

The Big Sur Marathon was a blast, and the course was easily the most beautiful I'd ever run. It was a dream come true running alongside friends in such a gorgeous landscape on a perfect California day. After we managed to find each other in the finish area craziness, we spent the rest of the day savoring Carmel and Monterey, eating delicious food, drinking good wine, and enjoying the kind of camaraderie only true friends share. It was the trip of a lifetime with the best people. But even as I soaked in the beauty of the day, I couldn't shake the feeling that my time was running out. Sitting on the patio of our winery Airbnb, a glass of wine in hand, I knew what had to come next. It was time to address my knees. The fun had to stop at least temporarily. I had to stop running, face the reality of my knees' failure, and find a solution. My goal wasn't just to keep running; it was to get my Six Star in Tokyo, and I couldn't afford to push through the pain anymore.

Now, when I say, "stop running," I mean "cut back." It wasn't going to be an immediate halt, but rather a gradual process. I reduced my mileage slowly, shaving a mile here, and another there. Running five miles instead of six. Four miles instead of five. Then three, just a few times a week. Finally, I came to a stop. To keep my cardio up, I picked up my road bike again and kept on swimming, but it wasn't the same. I missed my BRFs, our early morning runs, our sunrises, and the rhythms of our conversations that made the miles fly by. But once again, the goal shifted. My health had to come first. The running would be there when the time was right but only if I took care of my body now.

My long-time chiropractor recommended seeing a pain management doctor. Not pain management with drugs but with tools to reduce inflammation, increase blood flow, and repair tissues and cartilage. All the things that actually address the problem but incidentally insurance doesn't cover. Go figure.

Dr. Knabb was unlike other doctors I had encountered. He wore khakis and plaid shirts instead of a white coat. He never kept me waiting and never rushed out the door to the next patient. He always sat down face to face and looked me in the eye when he talked. He didn't insist I stop running but instead offered to help figure out a way to get me back doing the activities I loved. No judgment, only curiosity. He also cursed a lot, which I found funny and endearing.

"Not being able to run is bullshit," he said. "We will do everything we can so you can do the things you enjoy."

We started off with a plan to use electromagnetic transduction therapy (EMTT) to stimulate blood flow and cell growth. This noninvasive and painless procedure helped to not only increase blood flow but spur tissue growth to the affected area, my knees. I sat in a chair in a closed room with a ring between my knees while it sent out EMTT vibes. Easy peasy. Next, we added shockwave therapy. Not so easy peasy. He had warned me that this could be a painful treatment that really depended on my threshold for pain. The higher levels of shockwave they could send through my knees, the more effective the result. This seemed intimidating, but I wanted results. My first session was excruciating, and my pulse dropped to thirty-two, so we had to stop the procedure before I passed out. It felt like torture, and I would have rather passed out! The next round, I drank more water ahead of time and felt prepared to deal with the pain since I knew what was coming my way. It went somewhat better, but we just couldn't get the machine levels high enough to see major results. We kept at it for several more weeks, but my pain tolerance could not withstand the level of shockwave therapy needed to see progress.

"Can you just keep doing the shock therapy while I'm passed out? That way, you can increase it to the max level, and I won't feel anything," I asked. Megan, the physical therapist, looked at me in horror.

"Runners are the only people that would ask that question." She shook her head. "We will not shockwave you while you're passed out." It doesn't hurt to ask.

Dr. Knabb recommended I consider platelet-rich plasma (PRP) therapy. The procedure involved drawing large amounts of my own blood, spinning it at high speeds to separate the components, and isolating the "super cells" that promote healing and blood flow. Dr Knabb then would use sonogram technology to inject the plasma into the affected areas of my knee, aiming to stimulate repair and encourage cell growth in the meniscus and kneecap areas. The treatment had mixed reviews for knees, but Dr. Knabb assured me that many of his patients had seen positive results with PRP. Not surprisingly, the treatment didn't come cheap, and insurance didn't cover it. I dove into clinical trials and scoured every online resource I could find, hesitant to invest thousands of dollars in a treatment that might not work. Yet, I found myself running out of options. I longed to return to running, and if PRP offered a path back, I decided I should take the leap.

The next few weeks were all about nourishing my body in every way I could. I stocked up on spinach, leafy greens, and other nutrient-packed foods, making sure I was fueling my body with the best possible ingredients. Hydration became a priority. Plenty of water, all day, every day. My focus wasn't just on the physical act of healing but on creating the ideal internal environment to support it. I wanted my blood to have the highest platelet count, thinking that every little bit would help speed up recovery and encourage healing.

Was it science or superstition? Maybe a bit of both. I didn't have concrete evidence it would make a huge difference, but I needed to feel like I was doing everything in my power to set myself up for success.

In late June of 2023, Dr. Knabb performed the PRP treatment, which turned out to be nearly painless. The biggest challenge came from getting enough blood out of my small veins, which didn't like giving up blood easily. Dr. Knabb drew my blood himself a rarity, as I don't think I'd ever had a doctor do that before. Then again, he wasn't like other doctors. He said I had an exceptionally high platelet count on the day of the procedure, and I couldn't help but smile and mentally high-five myself. I was finally winning at something. Lying on the table with monitors beeping around me, I watched as Dr. Knabb injected the plasma into various parts of both knees. I could actually see it seeping into my tissues, and I repeated a mantra in my head: "Heal my tissues, my cartilage, my arthritis, and even my meniscus!"

After about fifteen minutes, he declared the job done, and I was free to go. Of course, walking and standing felt like a not-so-fun game of "let's see how much pain I can endure." Dr. Knabb advised me to rest for eight weeks and avoid running, but he said he would give me the green light to swim and bike soon. I followed his directions to the letter. I wasn't about to risk doing anything prematurely and ruining my chance at recovery. I also had a master plan brewing that focused on losing body weight to ease the pressure on my knees, getting stronger through resistance training, and fine-tuning my running form.

During our follow-up appointments, I kept up with the EMTT, which Dr. Knabb assured me would boost cell growth and make the PRP work even better. As I lay there, I repeated my mantra, picturing my tissues connecting like puzzle pieces and healing. Gradually, the doctor allowed me to increase my walking regime as well as resume biking, swimming, and working out. I felt like a kid planning a secret mission, excited to put my recovery plan into action.

After the PRP, I dubbed it my "summer of working out." I hit the gym religiously, three to four days a week, cycling and swimming like I was training for the Olympics. I had a target date in late August when I could start running again, but I knew I had to ease back in to avoid any fresh injuries. Lifting weights and doing dynamic movements kept me motivated. My friend Molly joked that we were training like professional athletes. I was driven and determined, all while keeping an eye on the calendar because my marathon training program was set to kick off in November.

By late August 2023, I started run/walking on an anti-gravity treadmill, also known as the Alter-G. It is a high-tech, air-filled contraption that made me feel like I was running on air. I would step into the plastic "bubble," zip myself in with special shorts and be "lifted" by the mechanism, which reduced the weight pounding on the treadmill and my knees. At the time, only one Alter-G treadmill existed in Wilmington, and lucky for me, it sat at a physical therapy office just around the corner from my house. They offered a deal of five sessions for one hundred dollars. I jumped on it. It felt like the perfect way to gradually ease back into running without hitting the pavement. Plus, Dr. Knabb fully supported it, which made me feel even more confident about my high-tech bubble adventure.

In the early days of running on it, I gasped for breath and my body ached. When I set the treadmill to 70 percent, meaning it carried 30 percent of my weight, it felt almost too easy, like I was gliding through the air. But I knew better than to get too comfortable with that feeling. I understood that carrying my full weight would feel much different. Gradually, I bumped the setting up to 80 percent, then eighty-five, and eventually,

I removed all assistance and carried 100 percent of my weight. The Alter-G proved to be a fantastic tool for me to return to running while recovering from PRP. After eight weeks, I was eager to get back outside. I decided to make my running comeback on the track, knowing the surface would be softer than any roads. On August 10, I met my BRFs at the UNCW track, but barely managed to run for one minute. The heat and humidity made it tough, but I remained determined. I had missed my running buddies, and it meant the world to me that they were willing to "run" with me on my first day back after nearly four months. I felt completely out of shape despite my regular gym sessions, swimming, and biking. Running fitness was a totally different beast.

After my first outdoor run, I jotted down in my log, "At the track with my BRFs, feeling very out of shape, definitely harder than the treadmill. Did a run/walk and took it easy. A little pain at first, but it went away. A bit of achiness. Band-Aid ripped off!" I managed to run 2.38 miles in thirty-three minutes, averaging a pace of 13:59 min/mile. Not exactly breaking records, but I was back in the game.

To support my knees, I ordered Incrediwear knee sleeves, which Dr. Knabb recommended. They provided support and felt great, like a warm hug to both knees. They quickly became a staple in my running gear. Honestly, I felt like a superhero every time I slipped them on, like I was gearing up with a secret weapon. Every run started with those knee sleeves and had become an essential part of my routine.

While juggling PT exercises, visits to Dr. Knabb, swimming, biking, and now running, my knees held up, and I started running longer distances and gradually introduced more speed work. Now, I wouldn't call myself speedy. Rather, I was more like a tortoise in training but I was at least able to complete the workouts. Once again, inch by inch, my body adapted, and I was getting stronger.

Scott and I rarely ate out anymore, which allowed me to eat a cleaner, higher-protein diet. Salmon, shrimp, salads, and a rainbow of veggies became my staple foods. I barely touched alcohol, a significant shift from my party-loving forties. Prioritizing sleep became my new mantra because, after all, that's when the recovery magic happens. I was on a mission, more focused than I'd ever been since I started running. My secret goal? To run a personal best in my last Six Star race in Tokyo. Determination oozed from my pores with every workout.

I kept up my swimming and cycling to maintain cardio fitness while gradually increasing my running. Two and a half miles turned into three, then four. I transitioned from running two or three days a week to four, and I started logging my mileage again. Ten miles a week turned into fifteen. Sure, my knees sometimes hurt, but I ran through it. In time, the pain began to fade, and I grew stronger, faster, and recovered more quickly after each run.

At a party, I bumped into Dr. Knabb.

"Your knees will continue to heal for at least a year," he told me. Hearing that filled me with happiness. It felt like I was truly on the path to recovery, and I couldn't wait to discover just how strong I could become.

My total mileage for September was 59.87 miles. I hadn't logged that many miles since April, right after Big Sur. In October, I ramped up to running four days a week and worked toward a six-mile-long run. I hit that goal on October 7 at the Run for the Ta Tas 5K, where I added a three-mile warm-up before the race. On weekends, I slowly increased my mileage and incorporated longer runs. My target was a ten-mile-long run by early November. I tackled speed work at the track on Thursdays, but I kept it within limits since there was no need to make my knees audition for a horror movie. By the end of October, I clocked in at 90.75 miles. I made sure to keep one day a week as a complete rest day, and I swam on my active recovery days. Sure, my knees still had a bit of a grumpy attitude, but I kept them in check with acupuncture when needed. Often, I ran early in the morning before work, then headed to the gym in the evenings. This allowed my body time to recover from the run while building strength and kept my rest days truly restful.

Then came Saturday, November 4, the date I tackled my first ten-mile-long run in nearly eight months. It was a perfect day to reach this milestone, coinciding with our quarterly "Running of the Clubs," where all the local running clubs in Wilmington gathered at our favorite local brewery, Waterman's. We ran to Wrightsville Beach toward a popular resort on the north end. My log that day read, "Perfect weather could've dressed lighter, great group, nice headwind going toward Shell Island, little warm coming back. I wanted to stop at eight miles but kept going. Knees hurt BAD!"

I finished ten miles at a 10:57/mile pace, completing the run in one hour and forty-eight minutes. The next day, I swam and let my legs float behind me, imagining my tissues repairing and rejuvenating as if they were on a relaxing vacation. Hitting this milestone truly made me feel like I had rejoined the running world. I still felt pain, but I could manage it. Little by little, I regained my confidence.

November 6, the following Monday, marked a turning point. My log that day noted I hadn't slept well but had woken up ready to run. My legs and knees felt strong, and I was looking forward to my friend Diana joining us for the first time. Conditions were perfect; the weather stayed cool and I dressed spot-on for the temperature. Our group clicked, which made for an enjoyable run. I ran 5.27 miles at a 10:47 pace, not fast by any means, but something shifted for me during those miles. Sometimes, a run simply feels different, whether it's because you have more energy or your fitness training kicks in, and that morning, I felt stronger in my entire body including shoulders, arms, core, legs, knees, and even my feet. And just in time. The first day of Tokyo Marathon training began a week later, on November 13, 2023.

I found myself on a camping trip north of Raleigh, where the terrain rolled with hills. To my surprise, I powered up the hills without feeling winded. In fact, Bodie lagged behind, struggling to keep pace. I credited this newfound strength to my gym sessions lifting heavy weights, pushing a sled, flipping tires, and crushing squat after squat.

I decided not to use a coach for this marathon cycle. Confident in my own abilities, I knew exactly what to focus on in terms of fitness and nutrition. Crafting a training plan that combined speed work, tempo runs, hill repeats, and long runs, each workout designed to push me forward in the most efficient way possible. While I had always used the run/walk method for marathons, I secretly aimed to run every single mile of this race. I wasn't ruling out walking, but I was determined to do my best, with consistent effort.

What is the most surprising perk of training for the Tokyo Marathon? The cold, gloomy winter! The mornings were dark and chilly, but that only meant I could run in the crisp, refreshing air. Compared to northern climes, winter in Wilmington was like a mild escape and ideal for marathon training. Every run was a breath of fresh air, literally and figuratively. During the first week of training, I cut back on my mileage, and I welcomed the lighter load like a warm cup of cocoa. Many runners dove straight into high mileage, but I preferred to ease in. That week, I ran a five-mile race as part of my long run, with one simple goal: keep my pace under ten minutes per mile. I warmed up slowly with a three-mile jog, held a steady pace during the race, and ended up snagging second place in my age group with little to no pain. By the end of November, I had logged a solid 97.76 miles. My knees even cheered me on!

My training plan called for hill repeats every Tuesday. Hill repeats often felt like a love-hate relationship. While they built leg strength and mental toughness, they also felt like being chased by a serial killer. I sprinted up a hill as fast as I could, then recovered on the downhill. The goal? Get faster with each repeat. I enjoyed this workout because I could see my times getting a second or two quicker each week. My glutes definitely got the message. Hello, muscle activation.

My training partners would show up at 6:00 a.m. to run with me most mornings and ask, "What is on your plan today?"

"Tempo with surges," I'd say. Surges were accelerations for about a hundred meters during a run. These workouts changed each week, which kept things fresh and prevented boredom. Running can easily turn into a snooze-fest, so mixing it up kept all of us engaged. Coach Rhonda had taught me to make the last mile the best mile during long runs, so I always aimed to make my final stretch my fastest, simulating a strong finish. My training partners incorporated this motto into their training methods, too. We pushed each other to run harder and faster on our speed days.

Flipping through my logbook, it was clear I had been working my tail off. Four days of running each week, three days in the gym, swimming, and yoga for active recovery. It was a schedule that kept me busy but also kept me moving forward. My friends had noticed how quickly I bounced back from the PRP treatment after all those months off, and I credited my progress to the consistent effort I'd put in at the gym and in the pool. By the end of December, I had logged a solid 130.59 miles. As I closed out the month, I wrote in my log, "Another year of running! So happy to be able to get stronger and tackle these workouts!" It felt like a small victory, not just in terms of the miles, but in the progress made through the challenges.

While cruising through my marathon buildup, I researched and planned our trip to Japan. I didn't know anyone who had been there, so I dove into a couple of Facebook travel groups like a tourist in a gift shop, eager to soak up all the advice. We knew we wanted to stay for two weeks to make the most of the long journey, especially with a whopping twelve-hour time difference to contend with.

I would tell Scott, "Japan is so big; how can we see everything in two weeks?" He would roll his eyes.

"Please don't drag us around the entire country. Pick a couple of places so we can relax and take it in and actually enjoy the vacation." Wise words. Trying to see all the incredible places in Japan in one trip would take at least a year. I booked a hotel in Tokyo's financial district, conveniently located just a half mile from Tokyo Station, a major subway and train hub in the heart of the city. We could walk to the station, the Imperial Palace, and, most importantly, the finish line of my marathon. Priorities! Japan unfolded like a giant buffet of sights and experiences, making it tough to narrow down an itinerary without feeling like we were on a whirlwind tour. I wanted to find somewhere relaxing after the marathon chaos, so I set my sights on Hakone, a picturesque lake region about ninety minutes outside Tokyo. Mt. Fuji stole the spotlight, with views so spectacular they could've come straight out of a postcard. I booked a hotel on Lake Ashinoko, offering breathtaking vistas and a ferry landing right next door. Famous for its hot springs and stunning natural beauty, this area provided exactly the serene escape we wanted after the hustle and bustle of Tokyo.

Next on my list came Kyoto. As a history buff, I felt drawn to the area, knowing it's one of Japan's oldest cities, largely untouched by the destruction of World War II. I spent months immersed in research, reading articles, binge-watching YouTube travel videos, and meticulously plotting where to stay. I asked endless questions in travel groups as I wanted to stray off the beaten path to uncover the "real Japan." The excitement grew and this trip was shaping up to be unforgettable.

As the New Year rolled in, my training hit new highs, and it felt like my body was transforming right before my eyes. Marathon training works in mysterious ways. One week, you're struggling to keep up, and the next, you're nailing distances at paces you never thought possible. Any seasoned runner will tell you that this is a universal truth, whether you're a weekend warrior or an elite marathoner.

I kept a sharp focus on my diet, loading up on protein after those grueling workouts to aid recovery. My meals often looked like a rainbow, packed with vibrant vegetables, and I had drastically cut back on alcohol down to about one drink a month. Who was this person I had become? It was a far cry from the party-animal version of myself, the one who could barely muster the energy to run thirty seconds on a treadmill. The changes weren't just physical. Even though I had slimmed down and could feel the difference in my knees on every run, losing weight also made each step, in my mind, seem more manageable, which mentally fortified me for the road ahead.

Every morning, I pampered my feet like royalty, soaking them in Epsom salts and slipping into Sheryl's Normatec boots that I had borrowed for a daily dose of recovery. The boots boosted blood flow to my legs, easing the tension that built up from both the miles and the stress of everyday life. Marathon training was a selfish pursuit, and I fully embraced it. My life outside of running took a backseat, and my training partners probably saw more of me than my family did. I juggled a demanding full-time sales career with a manager who thrived on creating drama. I found solace in running. It once again became my escape and my therapy. Venting with my BRFs after tough days at work allowed me to channel frustration into something positive. With each mile, I built resilience not just in my legs but in my ability to endure the challenges of my job. Running became the counterbalance to the turmoil at work, a way to recalibrate.

Amid all of this, Scott still grappled with his own battle: chronic jaw pain that made the simplest tasks, like eating, a challenge. But despite the constant discomfort, his determination never waned. He committed to joining me in Japan for the Tokyo Marathon, to stand by my side when I earned my Six Star Medal. His unwavering support reminded me that no matter how tough the journey got, I didn't have to face it alone. The promise of sharing that moment with him kept me going when things felt crushing.

Track workouts in January unfolded with a whirlwind of eight-hundred-meter repeats, each one feeling like a mini battle. We kicked off at a half marathon pace and steadily pushed ourselves to a 5K pace, watching our fitness skyrocket with every lap. The track became our proving ground, where we made the most significant strides. Each week, I both eagerly anticipated and dreaded those grueling sessions, reminding myself it was just forty-five minutes of hard work before I could collapse and check it off my list. Having friends like Mike and Tracy #4 (yes, we had so many Tracys, we had to number them) made a world of difference. They were my "rabbits," spurring me on as we tackled those fast-paced intervals together. We braved wild, blustery mornings on the track, where the wind howled like a banshee, but every gust only fueled my resilience and grit for race day. I couldn't help but chuckle as I heard T-4 swearing in her thick New Jersey accent, her frustration rising as we fought against the relentless headwind yet still met our pace goals.

The day of the first eighteen-mile-long run arrived, the distance that had haunted me as my personal nemesis for so long. This time, I would conquer it and relinquish those negative thoughts. The morning greeted me with a gusty wind as the run began at 6:00 a.m. from our favorite coffee shop, It's Coffee Time. A few pre-miles were logged before the official group run started at 7:00 a.m. Luckily, the "OG" Tracy stuck by my side for the entire distance. Despite feeling crampy and dehydrated, we powered through, finishing strong. The last mile turned out to be our best, and we clocked three hours and eleven minutes at 10:37 per mile. That eighteen-mile monkey? Finally gone.

Marathon training is like a never-ending game of "How Far Can You Go Without Actually Going There?" Each week, I built up my long runs, peaking at twenty to twenty-two miles. Running the full 26.2 miles in training was like trying to eat an entire pizza in one sitting: possible, but you'll regret it later. While elite runners might go the distance in training, the rest of us mere mortals should save our legs for race day. The recovery required after completing a full marathon in training far outweighed the benefit. Instead, I ran thirty to forty-five miles per week, gradually building my endurance without the need to run the full 26.2 miles before race day. We also had "down weeks," which basically meant, "Let's let you recover, but still make you work hard!" During these weeks, long-run-mileage dropped for recovery, but speed and tempo workouts ramped up. It felt like a cruel joke more intensity but with a side of relaxation. It's all a mental game.

To test my fitness, I decided to run the Charleston Half Marathon on January 20, 2024, in Charleston, South Carolina. It felt like the perfect excuse to race through the charming streets of Charleston and to get my running buddies signed up as well. We were pumped to take in the sights along the famous Battery and the Citadel, admiring the stunning architecture and historic homes. The thought of racing through such a picturesque city had us all excited and ready to take on the challenge. We stayed near the start line so we could roll out of bed and waltz over to the race. But when we arrived on Friday, the weather turned cold and windy, and I started to worry we'd be racing in a wind tunnel, unable to hit my goals. I wanted to start strong at marathon pace for the first ten miles and then gradually pick it up for the last three, essentially a fast finish that would simulate race day. Race morning came on Saturday, cold but miraculously not windy. My friend Brad graciously offered to run with me, acting as my personal pace keeper, while Mike and T-4 were gunning for a sub-two-hour half marathon. Molly and Jenelle just wanted to have a good time and finish together.

We lined up at the start, snapping photos and bouncing around like a bunch of kids waiting for the school bus. We all checked our bags so we could dive into our post-race warm clothes like they were cozy security blankets after the race. As the sun peeked over the horizon, we shuffled into the corrals, and with a bang, we were off! Brad, my trusty running sidekick, chatted away, keeping me entertained during the first ten miles. He counted them down and informed me of my pace. I'm not much of a talker during a race, so I soaked in the scenery while he kept the conversation flowing like a river. We high-fived Mike and T-4 during an out-and-back section. Approaching mile ten, Brad suggested picking up the pace, but I was already there, soaring like a caffeinated gazelle, in my mind at least. I cranked up my music, stretched out my stride, and let the rhythm take over. The world around me blurred as I slipped into the zone focused, locked in, and ready to go. I could hear Brad chatting, but what he was saying didn't register. The last mile came at me like a storm: my hands freezing, the wind howling, but I wasn't about to slow down. I pushed harder, every ounce of energy focused on the finish line.

Then, there it was. I crossed the finish line with a massive grin, heart pounding, adrenaline surging. My time? 2:14:39, with a negative split. I had crushed my goal, and in that moment, it felt like everything clicked into place. The sweat, the effort, the sacrifice it all paid off. The high was overwhelming, and the sense of accomplishment felt amazing. My knees held up; I was gaining fitness and would only improve going forward. The race fueled my confidence. If I could nail a race with good weather, then a personal best in Tokyo was totally in the cards. My goals were coming into focus like a newly sharpened pencil, and I was all in.

The next month flew by like a caffeinated squirrel. I tackled hard workouts, cross-trained like a pro, and recovered like a boss, ready to kick off each week with renewed enthusiasm. I finished January with an impressive 144.09 miles and February with 121.57 miles. These numbers felt like a nostalgic trip back to my glory days. My knees were holding up beautifully, and everyone, including me, was stunned at how well the training was going. It was like I was running on a cloud of optimism, with maybe a sprinkle of fairy dust for good measure. As I wrapped up the final details for our Japan trip, I dove into the marathon taper process. After months of training like a beast, the two weeks leading up to the race forced me to slow down. The goal? Let my body heal from all the mileage, but it became a mental challenge. While I typically looked forward to tapering, by the second week, doubts began to creep in. *Can I really run a marathon after barely hitting twelve miles in the past two weeks?*

I reminded myself that this was all part of the plan a recovery period, not a sign of losing fitness. The last track workout on the 27th of February felt like a revelation. Three by eight-hundred-meter repeats at a 5K pace came effortlessly, each one feeling like I was flying. Running 7:50, 7:23, and 7:15 paces, numbers I hadn't seen since London training were almost too easy. The thought of smashing my personal record blared in my head like an overenthusiastic cheerleader. Not only was Tokyo and the Six Star within reach, but a personal best as well.

Chapter 17 – Tokyo Marathon 2024

A t 5:45 a.m. in Tokyo, the earth started rumbling and shaking. In our hotel room, the hangers in the closet swished back and forth, their rhythm unsettling. Scott and I stared at each other. It felt as if we were being tossed around on a shaky carnival ride.

"What's happening?" Scott asked, eyes wide.

"I think it's an earthquake," I said, voice panicked. "What do we do?" Scott started pacing around the room, unsure whether we should head into the hallway. I vaguely recalled hearing that you should stand in a doorway during an earthquake, but I wasn't sure if that was outdated advice or worth following.

My phone blew up with text notifications. Our running group chat exploded with frantic messages: "EARTHQUAKE!" "Did you feel that?" We were on the eleventh floor, clueless about what to do. Our eyes met, wide with disbelief, as we hoped it wouldn't escalate. I recalled the devastating earthquake in Western Japan on the Noto Peninsula just eight weeks before, on January 1, 2024. Two hundred eighty-one people died, and over six hundred were injured, with trillions of dollars in damage. The last thing any of us wanted was for this shaky adventure to cancel the race or worse, kill us all.

Thankfully, the tremor slowly started to ease, the rumbling coming to a stop as if nothing had happened. I placed my hand on my chest, unsure how to process my first earthquake experience. Turning on the news, we learned it had been a 5.2 magnitude quake about seventy-five miles southeast of Tokyo. Earthquakes are common in Japan, sitting as they do on the infamous "Ring of Fire" a seismic hotspot prone to earthquakes, tsunamis, and volcanic eruptions. Oh my, welcome to Japan!

Tokyo spanned roughly 240 square miles, yet it stood as the most densely populated city on Earth, with forty-one million people in the metro area. Race organizers designed a route to minimize disruption, starting in a government building complex on a Sunday. About 60 percent of the course consisted of out-and-back sections where runners ventured out for a set distance and then turned around to retrace their steps. For a sprawling city like Tokyo, this layout minimized the need for extensive road closures, unlike races in cities like

New York where vast swaths of the population could be affected by shutting down a single bridge or avenue.

We left on the 28th of February, a Wednesday, and arrived in Tokyo on Thursday, the 29th, around 3:00 p.m. I had splurged on premium economy bulkhead seats for the extra legroom, which was basically the best seat behind first class. The journey was surprisingly smooth, and although I didn't get much sleep, I managed to rest and hydrate while starting my carb-loading mission.

A group of about eight runners from Wilmington were headed to Japan for the marathon, and our group text erupted with excitement as we shared our travel adventures. Once Scott and I landed, we tackled the train system like seasoned pros (or so we claimed) and stumbled a few blocks to our hotel, still trapped in the fog of jet lag. After checking in, we spotted a 7-Eleven across the street because, when in Japan, right? We grabbed a simple dinner in our room, and by 7:30 p.m., we surrendered to exhaustion, living our best "we're on vacation" lives.

After the seismic excitement the next morning, Scott and I enjoyed a relaxed breakfast at our hotel. Breakfast in Japan was a delightful mix of surprises. The buffet offered soup, salad, roasted veggies, and even desserts like key lime pie. We chose some undercooked scrambled eggs, and, as we found out, raw eggs are normal in Japan. We also indulged in croissants, pastries, and all sorts of baked treats.

Meanwhile, Scott struggled to eat. It took him at least an hour to finish a meal. I watched as he engaged in a determined struggle with his food. It was as if he were in a slow-motion eating contest, taking an eternity to consume each morsel. Since he couldn't talk when eating, he had mastered the art of silence during meals, nodding as I babbled on like a chatty news anchor.

Despite the jet lag wrapping around us like a wet blanket, we bravely set out to tackle Tokyo's labyrinthine train and bus system, armed only with Google Translate and Google Maps, our modern-day navigational wizards. First up on our adventure was the teamLab Planets experience, followed by a pilgrimage to the marathon expo to collect my race packet.

A fun and immersive artistic experience, teamLab Planets charmed us. We laughed as we explored the amazing sights, sounds, and feels of the museum. The exhibits ranged from simple, huge colored balls to intricate orchids and flowers arranged in a steamy greenhouse, the plants gliding up and down as we walked through. We found it to be a unique and wonderful place.

I had decided to keep my plans light in Tokyo to avoid exhausting my legs, but that didn't mean I wasn't up for some exploration. We hopped onto the subway, then a bus, embarking on a forty-minute journey to the Tokyo Big Sight building, the location of the marathon expo. After leaving Scott in a coffee shop, I entered the colossal and uniquely designed convention center, instantly swept into the organized chaos of race packet pick-up. It felt like a well-orchestrated ballet of runners and volunteers.

As I queued up, the line snaked endlessly up escalators and down long hallways, with enthusiastic volunteers guiding us like friendly beacons of light. When I reached the main hall, I found yet another line for my bib and running essentials. The anticipation was palpable, almost electric.

But like any good marathon expo, the excitement didn't stop at packet pick-up. I had heard whispers on the Facebook World Marathon Majors page about the scarcity of Tokyo gear, and sure enough, when I made it to the merchandise area, it felt like a treasure hunt gone awry. The shelves seemed to mock me, displaying only a few lonely items. No T-shirts, singlets, hats, or any other clothing. In the end, I settled for some socks, a buff, and an adorable Tokyo bear, my new cuddly companion for the journey ahead. But alas, the elusive finisher jacket was nowhere to be found, leaving me a bit deflated. I had a collection from each race, and missing this one felt like missing a medal after crossing the finish line.

Once I made it through the race gear gauntlet, I entered the vibrant main expo area. Vendors beckoned like carnival barkers, inviting me to play games, snap photos, or partake in clever marketing stunts designed to lure me into their booths. Out on the show floor, I stumbled upon some fun Tokyo Marathon memorabilia, but my primary mission was to visit the Abbott World Marathon Majors booth. I wanted to see that coveted medal one last time before it would finally rest around my neck.

At the booth, I received a special bib to wear on my back, boldly proclaiming that I was running for my sixth star. The staff also handed me directions for how to claim my medal post-race. They informed me that thousands of runners were chasing their sixth star, and two tents would be set up at the finish area to accommodate all the star-seekers. The thought that I would finally be part of this exclusive club was exhilarating.

My friend Sami, a local Wilmington coach and IRONMAN race director, and I planned to run a short shakeout run around the Imperial Palace on Saturday. We had shared the same running circles for years, but while I ran half marathons and marathons, Sami conquered triathlons and racked up IRONMAN finishes in Kona. The air was chilly, and the wind nipped at us, making me second-guess my race day outfit for the zillionth time. I jotted down in my log, "Feeling good, not too creaky. I think I'm ready. Imperial Palace, 7 AM, 3.47 miles, 10:48 pace." We wrapped up with a couple of selfies to document our adventure. The run was just what I needed a brief but refreshing reminder that I had put in the work and was ready for what was ahead.

Meanwhile, I had been carb-loading like a beast, and Japan turned out to be a carb-lover's paradise. The locals had a serious sweet tooth, and the variety of pastries, desserts, and breads mesmerized me. But it wasn't just the sweet treats; those glorious rice balls were my carb-loading dream. Little pockets of heaven, available at every 7-Eleven, became my ultimate fuel for the race, not to mention the egg sandwiches and ready-made pancakes, all perfect pre-race fuel.

The night before the race, I went all out, stocking up on salted rice balls, chicken on a stick, and a piece of sourdough bread. I was practically bursting with carbs and excitement, feeling both physically fueled and mentally prepared for race morning. I couldn't help but think, *If carbs were a superpower, I'd be invincible right now.*

Sami traveled to Japan as part of a marathon tour group, and they graciously invited me to tag along on race morning, sparing me the headache of navigating the Tokyo subway system to the start line. Major lifesaver. The previous day, I wrestled with the underground maze, only to end up in tears of frustration. After studying endless signs labeled "Exit" and still not knowing which way to go, I gave up and took a taxi. Honestly, the subway stations felt like trying to decipher ancient hieroglyphs; every time I thought I'd found the right exit, I ended up three miles off course. Following Sami's group on race morning changed everything. I could relax, soak in the buzz around me, and follow their group leader without worrying about getting lost. The trip to the start line felt effortless, stress-free and a huge sense of relief washed over me.

From the moment we landed in Japan, the efficiency amazed us. From customs and immigration to the subway and train schedules, everything ran like a well-oiled machine. Bag check took no time at all. Finding our corral felt like a walk in the park, and the lines for the porta-johns practically didn't exist. The race organizers choreographed every detail, ensuring everything unfolded with the precision of clockwork.

Speaking of clockwork, the Japanese prided themselves on punctuality to a fault. If you show up five minutes early, you're late. The pre-race athletic guide hammered home the importance of timeliness, and the cutoff times left no room for negotiation. No excuses. If you didn't meet the time limits, race officials pulled you from the course without ceremony. Volunteers were assigned to "sweep" those falling behind, ensuring no one lingered. I could only imagine how nerve-wracking it must be for those runners anxiously eyeing the clock, the weight of possible failure pressing down on them. The heartbreak of not finishing surely weighed heavily on them. To top it all off, the athletic guide resembled an eighteen-page tome of rules and etiquette. Japanese culture, steeped in respect for tradition and order, demanded that every participant adhere to these regulations. They followed them with precision, It was like gearing up for a marathon within a tightly calibrated matrix. I felt a mix of excitement and intimidation, eager to be part of it but wary of the exacting standards. I wanted to respect every rule, but there was a little devil perched on my shoulder, whispering temptations to bend or break just one or two. I could almost hear its mischievous laugh: *Come on, one tiny infraction won't hurt.*

Throwaway clothes went into designated bins before the race, no trash allowed on the ground, and runners couldn't pee anywhere except in a porta-john. Break that rule, and you were out. Then came the no-water rule. No handheld bottles, no hydration packs. Nothing. This one bothered me the most. I've always carried my own water to avoid the madness of aid stations and to stay hydrated on my terms. With no water stations for the first three miles, I already found myself sweating bullets about hydration. Much discussion ensued on the Facebook World Marathon Majors Challenge page.

"Why can't we bring a water bottle?" people would write.

"Their race, their rules," people would respond. We all found this rule hard to understand, and many sought to sneak in their own water bottle, but despite the devil on my shoulder, I ultimately adhered to the race rules.

As we shuffled around, the gun fired for the elite runners, and the buzz of anticipation filled the air. Our corral inched forward toward the start line, and suddenly, the rebellious urge surged within me. Without thinking, I veered off from the group.

"Where are you going?" they yelled.

"One last porta stop," I yelled back. "Have a great race!" I hopped over a barricade and darted into a nearby porta-john for one last bathroom break. I couldn't help but grin. I felt like a total radical. Tossing my throwaway clothes onto a bench (I know, I know rules!), I slipped back into the corral surrounded by complete strangers. The sun blazed brightly and the temperature hovered around forty degrees, and not a whisper of wind. Perfect race day weather. It felt like no time at all before we reached the start line. I pressed "start" on my watch and crossed the timing mats under the full sun. With fresh legs and cool weather, I felt like I could fly but I kept myself in check, knowing better than to push too hard too soon. By the time we reached the first water station at mile three, my throat was dry and I longed for a drink. I knew I'd feel slightly dehydrated throughout the race, but to manage the situation, I had to stick to their hydration timetable sipping either water or Pocari Sweat (their version of Gatorade) on their terms, not mine.

Since most of the Tokyo Marathon route were out-and-backs, I actually enjoyed it. It gave me the chance to spot both the speedy gazelles up ahead and the determined tortoises on the other side of the road. Many runners hated out and backs and preferred point-to-point to change up the scenery. I loved seeing huge, six-lane roads completely covered in runners.

Water stations were crazy and, frankly, annoying. Runners would dart left to get hydration, then swing right to get out of the way. Volunteers diligently picked up trash as cups and water flew in all directions, causing absolute mayhem. It wasn't until days later that I discovered the water stations had numbers corresponding to our bibs. We were supposed to go to the water station section number that matched the first number on our bib. Oops! I missed that detail in my intense study of those eighteen pages of rules and restrictions.

At some aid stations, older Japanese gentlemen held small plastic grocery bags. As the race went on, I realized they were collecting gel wrappers and other trash from runners. The detail felt so very Japanese charming, yet unrealistic, with over thirty thousand runners discarding mountains of trash throughout the day.

Much of the race kept us in direct sunlight, and while the temperatures were cool, the sun was intense. I started conserving energy in the sunlight and picking up the pace whenever I ran in the shade. The crowds were absolutely incredible, brimming with enthusiasm and cheer, even though I couldn't understand a word. The volunteers showered us with kindness and smiles of encouragement.

The athlete guide had detailed where the photographers would be stationed, so I made sure to channel my inner diva for the cameras. Looking back at the photos later, it felt like watching a mini-drama unfold: the early shots were all smiles and excitement, while the later ones displayed the classic marathon agony of sweat, grit, and determination.

As I crossed each timing mat, I blew kisses to Scott and my running pals, who tracked my every step. I was having a fantastic run and fully aware of it. No run/walk strategy this time; I committed to running the whole race. The course was flat and pristine. No potholes, cracks, indentations, or seams. Quite the contrast to the streets of New York.

As we weaved through the city, the towering high-rises of Tokyo dominated the skyline, but the Asakusa district really caught my eye. The massive temple and its five-story pagoda stood majestically, and I made a mental note to explore that area post-race. It looked enchanting. After Asakusa, I spotted the Tokyo Tower, which proudly claimed its title as the tallest tower in the world. And let's not forget the Asahi Building, often humorously dubbed the "golden turd." I think they were aiming for a flame design, but the result was . . . well, let's just say it was unforgettable.

I took some videos for my friends back home, capturing the electrifying energy of the streets packed with wall-to-wall runners from every corner of the globe. It was a breathtaking sight, and being part of this diverse crowd felt exciting. At mile twenty-one, I entered the last out-and-back stretch, and it was the cruelest kind of torture. We ran out for 1.95 miles, all while watching those on the other side of the street who were practically sprinting toward the finish.

I kept asking, *When's the turn? Where's the turn? Why is this taking so long?* I might have even thrown in a few colorful expletives for emphasis. Finally, after what felt like an eternity, we made the turn. We ran all the way back to the start of the out-and-back section, then took another turn, and the streets shifted to cobblestones. I couldn't see the finish line in the distance, but when I glanced at my watch, it ticked over to twenty-six miles. *What?* I kept running, pushing forward. Then, we turned right, and my watch flipped to twenty-seven miles. *What the hell?* We made another turn, and there it was, the finish line! I raised my hands in triumph as I crossed, my watch reading 27.08 miles. I couldn't believe it, but in that moment, I didn't care. I had earned my Six Star finisher status! I could feel it in my bones that I had run a personal best. My time: 4:41:48 a full minute and ten seconds faster than my first marathon in London eight years earlier.

I had come full circle. After battling injuries, gastrointestinal issues, fueling problems, heat, stress, and exhaustion in my other races, I applied everything I'd learned from those experiences, crafting new strategies and refining my techniques and it paid off. I felt incredibly proud. All the hard work I'd put in over the past eight months led me to this moment, and it had all been worth it.

In true Japanese fashion, the finish area unfolded with meticulous organization. Runners were grouped by the color of their bibs, making it easy to navigate to the bag drop and the World Marathon Majors tent. I quickly received my mylar blanket, medal, food, and the famous "robe" that volunteers gently draped over me as I wandered through the finish area. So many people congratulated me on my Six Star achievement, and before long, my emotions welled up, and tears started to form.

I approached the World Marathon Majors tent and completely broke down, a full-on ugly cry, with tears streaming down my face. The weight of moment, both the highs and the lows crashed down all at once. Huge victories, massive disappointments, injuries, cancer, hurricane, pandemic and now, finally, rising from the ashes with an incredible training cycle and a race that exceeded all expectations. Eight years of emotions poured out of me. I tried to collect myself for the photo op, but honestly, I felt like a hot mess. Happy, yes, but having a complete emotional meltdown.

Once the photos were done, I followed the sea of jubilant runners toward the underground subway station, a confusing and overwhelming maze even before running a marathon, my heart still racing from the adrenaline of crossing the finish line. After what felt like an eternity of ascending endless flights of stairs and navigating a tangle of gates, I burst into the daylight, gasping for breath and trying to regain my bearings. The trek to find Scott felt like an epic quest. Every step echoed the triumph and exhaustion coursing through me. And then, there he was. I dropped my gear like it was nothing and rushed into his embrace, feeling a surge of joy and relief. In that moment, all the struggles we had faced together melted away. He might not fully understand what drives me to chase these wild dreams, but I could see the pride in his eyes, a mirror of my own fierce determination. We had weathered storms together, and today, we had conquered the world.

The cold air bit at my skin as I quickly layered on warmer clothes. Together, we set off on the hike back to the hotel, the weight of my two medals feeling monumental around my neck. They clanged together like victory bells, amplifying my elation with each step. Strangers congratulated me on the Six Star achievement, their voices a chorus of encouragement. They shared their own marathon tales some on their third, fourth, or even fifth race. I felt a rush of kinship with them, urging them to keep pushing toward their goals, reminding them that every mile, and every challenge faced was a testament to their spirit. Today, I wasn't just a finisher; I was a warrior, and the battle had been worth every hard-fought step.

Back at the hotel, I sank into an Epsom salt bath, the warmth enveloping me like a comforting hug. After devouring snacks and downing my protein shake, I felt recharged and ready for nachos and champagne. We had pinpointed an American-style restaurant within walking distance from our hotel, a perfect post-marathon destination. Sitting around wasn't on my recovery agenda, and I knew staying mobile was key. As we chatted and feasted, I spotted a group of fellow marathon finishers still clad in their running kits, beers in hand, reliving the day's triumphs. I thought of my own running mates back home who had stayed up late to track my progress and shower me with congratulations. It warmed my heart to see Mike's 3:00 a.m. texts congratulating me.

In that moment of celebration, the realization hit: I had run a personal best on a certified course. My first and last marathons had become my fastest. I credited my debut performance to sheer enthusiasm and fresh legs, but the last one that was all about preparation, experience, and strategy. After seven marathons, I finally understood the delicate balance of fuel, training, and mental fortitude. Most importantly, I learned to surrender and have fun. Sure, I had goals, but after everything I'd endured, I realized that putting pressure on myself only stifled the joy of running.

Post-marathon recovery usually meant two weeks off, but after Tokyo, I felt spry. Maybe it was the pristine roads on the course or my countless gym workouts, but I couldn't wait to lace up and hit the pavement while visiting Hiroshima a week later. The pedestrian paths around the Peace Memorial Park and the riverside were runner friendly. I squeezed in a quick three-mile run on a cool morning, passing smiling locals out for their morning walks or lounging on benches. The city skyline reflected the morning light perfectly, making for a memorable run that I'll cherish for a long time. I finished as the famous Peace Clock Tower tolled its daily chime at 8:15 a.m., marking the moment the world experienced the first atomic bomb.

We headed back to Tokyo via bullet train and spent two more nights near Asakusa and the Tokyo Tower. Despite the cold rain, I ventured out to see as many sights as possible while Scott took a well-deserved rest. Our culinary adventure in Japan didn't unfold as I had hoped, thanks to his eating issues, but Asakusa charmed me with a treasure trove of tiny, unique restaurants tucked away in alleys some barely big enough for a table and a half. On the last day, I managed to find a small sushi restaurant, savoring each bite as though it were the last piece on Earth. I also snuck in one final run along the Sumida River, across from the Tokyo Tower, marveling at the rows of cherry trees poised to bloom in just a few weeks. The moment felt peaceful and reflective, the kind you treasure when the end of a long trip is within sight.

As we prepared to leave Japan, Scott and I reflected on the unforgettable trip we'd experienced. We had truly fallen in love with the country, the vibrant culture, the breathtaking landscapes, and the deep sense of history that pulsed through every corner. The efficiency of the transport system left us in awe. It felt like we were on a high-speed adventure every time we hopped on a train, moving through the country with pinpoint precision. Despite the language barrier, cab drivers, wait staff, and train employees went out of their way to help us, offering kindness and patience at every turn. It was as though Japan itself had wrapped us in a warm embrace. Every moment from the quiet temples to the bustling streets of Tokyo felt like a scene from a dream.

Our trip had been a perfect blend of breathtaking views, profound experiences, and the kind of hospitality that touches your soul. Japan had undoubtedly stolen a piece of our hearts, leaving us with memories that would linger long after we'd boarded the plane home.

After eight years, I became a Six Star Finisher.

Tokyo Marathon/Six Star Finisher, March 3, 2024

Chapter 18 – A Six Star Finisher

O nce home and settled back into normal life, reflections on the past eight years of this tumultuous journey flooded my mind. Scott and I had weathered storms that often felt insurmountable, transforming our lives completely. At one point, anger and resentment consumed me, and a longing for the days before cancer and jaw reconstruction; those simple, carefree days. A quote from motivational speaker Amy Purdy caught my eye: "Life doesn't need to go back to what it once was in order to be good."

The words struck a chord. They served as a poignant reminder that, although life had changed, it could still be rich and meaningful. Cultivating patience and releasing the rigid expectations about how life should unfold became essential. Some days felt easier than others, but the move toward acceptance would always be a work in progress.

The Six Star journey revealed profound truths and the immense power of community. Running alongside others, day in and day out, fostered a rare and beautiful intimacy. My running friends became my lifelines. They pushed me when I wanted to quit, inspired me with their own goals and triumphs, and grounded me when my thoughts began to spiral. They likely didn't realize the depth of their impact, especially since I often struggled to express those feelings. Scott, too, had served as my anchor. He reminded me to care for myself, urging me to sleep longer and rest more when I stubbornly ignored my body's signals. Through all the highs and lows, I understood the incredible strength that comes from connection and support. This journey changed me, but it also deepened my appreciation for the beauty of resilience and the bonds we form along the way.

Mission accomplished, life goal achieved, and comfort zone stretched. I had come a long way from that gangly, clumsy kid who never considered herself athletic. The days of overindulgence and questioning my relationship with alcohol lay behind me. I had surprised myself and probably shocked a few others by becoming an athlete in my mid-forties. It amazed me how small, everyday choices could accumulate into monumental, life-changing moments.

Everyone kept asking, "What's next?" now that I had hit this milestone. Honestly, I hadn't known at first. I just wanted to bask in the glory of my achievement without diving straight into another challenge. But let's face it peer pressure is a powerful beast. I'd likely be on the couch watching Netflix if it weren't for my fellow runners nudging me along. There's always someone itching to try a new race or tackle some absurd challenge. A few casual conversations, maybe a glass of wine, and before I knew it, we were signing up for the next big adventure.

There I was, eyeing a "sensible" half marathon trail race in the Virginia Highlands, nursing my knee after the PRP session, and staring down races ten months away. Naturally, I signed up and couldn't resist sending the link to my friends with an enthusiastic message: *Hey, let's do this in 2024*! Predictably, they were all in.

Then, the plot thickened. After a Saturday long run, they decided to up the ante and go for the 50K instead of the half marathon.

"What? I thought we were doing the half marathon?" I said to my running mates.

"We decided we might as well go for the 50K since we are driving all the way out there. By the way, the 50K is on Saturday, and the half marathon is on Sunday. We aren't going to stay and watch you race the half marathon."

They might disagree with my recounting, but that sparked me to get on my Ultra account and start scrolling.

"Sure, why not?" I said. "Let's go for it."

Mind you, I wasn't even running at that moment, but I jumped on the crazy train. Thirty-one miles. Absolutely bonkers, right?

The Grayson Highlands 50K trail race contained trails so steep and rugged they could give a mountain goat an inferiority complex. I soaked up my post-marathon glow for a week or two, but quickly realized I needed to jump back into training before I transformed into a full-fledged couch potato.

Back in Wilmington, I laced up my shoes and hit the trails with my friends. Before long, we were running like we'd signed up for survival school. Gone were the "marathon blues" I used to experience after a big race. Instead, I had a shiny new obsession to focus on because, clearly, thirty-one miles wasn't going to run itself.

Training for a trail race turned out to be a whole different running experience. First, we donned trail shoes with enough grip to conquer rocks, dirt, mud, and roots basically, human four-wheel drives. And, since my knees and I still had a *complicated* relationship, I decided to add trekking poles to my arsenal, especially for the downhill sections that always seemed to be my kryptonite. Fortunately, I had my friend Jennifer, a seasoned trail runner and all-around wizard, guiding me through the process. Her tips and encouragement were worth their weight in trail magic. Just when I thought I had this trail-running thing under control, I had a humbling setback. On a run through Uwharrie National Forest, I rolled my ankle so hard that it swelled up to the size of a grapefruit. My friend Mailyn had warned me that crying was a rite of passage when running in Uwharrie the first time, and I can confirm that was absolutely true. The trail was technical and rugged, and I had to hobble back toward the car, unsure if I could make it. At several points, I considered calling for an airlift rescue, but I continued dragging myself the five miles back to the parking lot, thoroughly frustrated and wondering if this 50K insanity was about to come to a screeching halt.

Back home, my chiropractor went to work on my ankle, and we added laser therapy to speed up the recovery process. I tried to keep weight off it as much as possible, which I found annoying. I had gone from running thirty miles a week to being immobile, which completely threw my brain and body off kilter. Putting on a shoe felt like a training event. Running was definitely out for at least a week.

Scott and I were on a camping trip two weeks before the race, and I thought, *Why not test the ankle?* I decided to try three miles just to see if I could make it without screaming in pain. Naturally, I roped in our camping friends for a little jog, figuring the distraction would help. The ankle definitely had a few things to say, but the pain stayed at a low simmer more like a polite conversation than a full-blown argument. Not exactly pain-free, but it was manageable enough to keep moving.

The next day, I was feeling a little daring, so I thought I'd push it to five miles. It was raining and cool, actually my favorite running conditions.

I told Scott, "I'm going to try and run five miles with Bodie and see how the ankle does."

I took my trusty sidekick along, and five miles felt so good that I opted for five more. When I finished, my ankle was a bit swollen, but I had just run ten miles! I felt invincible, like I could conquer this 50K after all. Our group wrapped up training, and the swelling in my ankle subsided. I started feeling stronger by the day. It was finally time to head to the mountains for the 50K.

We rented a huge house situated on top of a mountain outside of West Jefferson, North Carolina, with room for sixteen or seventeen of us. Arriving felt hectic as we all descended on the house with our running gear, hydration packs, snacks, trail shoes, and various special needs for the big day. My running partner, Mike, fed us a massive pasta meal, accommodating the gluten-free, vegetarians, vegans, and non-dairy folks.

The next morning, we had an early alarm to travel to Grayson Highlands State Park, just over the border in Virginia, about a forty-five-minute drive from the house. We woke up to a complete white-out fog so thick we had to get out of the car to see where to turn while coming down the mountain. It felt terrifying; we had no idea if the next turn would send our car tumbling down the side. After what felt like an eternity of white-knuckling our way to our destination, the fog still clung to the landscape, drizzle misting the air, and cold seeping into our bones while we milled around the start area. Perfect conditions for running in the woods all day when normal people would be snuggling up to a fire and drinking hot beverages.

Thanks to marathon training, my body had the endurance needed for a long day on the trails. Was I fast? Not even close. Did I discover that I had become a secret trail-running phenom? Absolutely not. The course proved brutal, with large rocks shifting underfoot and an elevation gain of five thousand feet. But we spotted ponies, longhorn steers, and baby cows, and the forest glowed with vibrant colors. Like the movie *Avatar*.

The first twenty-two miles of the race had been tough, but I felt good maybe a little too good. Striding into the aid station, I was on a high, joking with the volunteers that we flatlanders were absolutely crushing it and that we were rockstars. I should've known better. From mile twenty-three onward, it turned into pure hell. I'm sure the volunteers got a good laugh out of my bravado. Picture this: steep rock climbing alongside a beautiful waterfall that we couldn't even admire for fear of tumbling in. Then came the mud. Oh, the mud! Three or four miles of slippery madness, where every time I tried to run, my legs felt like they might launch me off my feet. And just when I thought things couldn't get worse, the last four miles of the race were an unrelenting uphill grind, where each step felt like a battle against gravity.

My mantra became my lifeline: *I'm going to be an ultra-runner; this is just temporary. Keep moving forward.* One foot in front of the other, over and over, until I spotted the finish line. My heart surged. *Yes! I made it!* But, in a twist of cruel irony, I was told we had to complete another two-mile loop.

"Two miles!" I yelled. On cue, it started pouring rain and the temperature dropped. I muttered a few choice words at the volunteer, which I later regretted. I'm sure they were just as miserable as we were.

Still, I rallied, as runners do. I tapped into my mantra: *I can do this; I will be an ultra-marathoner.* I kept repeating it like a prayer, determined to hit thirty-one miles when I crossed the line. Over and over, the words echoed in my mind, each one pushing me forward toward the end. Tears welled up as we crossed the finish line for real. I hugged my best running friends, my body soaked and shivering, but my heart swelling with pride. We had just completed a 50K. I could now proudly call myself an ultra-marathoner. How had that happened? I still had no idea, but in that moment, I was living proof that determination and a little bit of stubbornness could carry you across a finish line.

We returned to our cabin to a raucous welcome, complete with cheers and congratulations from our fellow runners seasoned veterans of crazy distances who made ultra-marathons look like a casual Sunday stroll. We toasted each other, reliving the day's wild adventures. Exhausted but elated, we were officially "ultra-marathoners!" Never in a million years had I imagined I'd take on something this challenging, but once again: never say never.

I'm sure many people think runners are a bit bonkers for willingly putting ourselves through such hardships. We push our bodies to the brink, turning our adventures into scenes straight out of a survival movie. But for me, it wasn't about proving how far I could stretch my limits but instead, the thrill of the adventure. Deep down, I still had that little kid inside me, eager to explore on foot, bike, skis, or any contraption that got my heart racing. Sure, I loved a tour bus ride, but there was an exhilarating freedom in using my own body to uncover hidden gems where no bus, car, or train could ever venture. The feeling of being vibrantly alive, soaking in every breathtaking view, and embracing the wildness of the world around us. So, here's to more adventures preferably with a little less mud and a lot more ponies!

After the 50K, even *more* people asked what I was going to do next. I had no answer. For the first time in over eight years, I found myself without a specific running goal looming over me. There were rumors floating around that the World Marathon Majors might add a seventh marathon, which became a reality when Sydney, Australia, was added as the seventh World Marathon Major. I would be lying if I didn't admit I had the itch to go after the newest World Majors addition and, in fact, did throw my name in the lottery. I didn't receive an entry, but it would've meant another summer training session and, well, we all know how I felt about doing that again.

What I know for sure is that I would keep exploring running alongside my BRFs and Bodie, showing up at the gym and the pool, and maybe even diving into new sports or activities I haven't yet discovered.

I think I have always known deep down, but now it has become crystal clear: there are no limits to what we can achieve if we set our minds to it. Stepping outside our comfort zones doesn't just feel necessary it can be fun, thrilling, and downright terrifying. It also becomes the place where we truly live. Each challenge presents a chance to embrace the wild ride of life, and I am there for every exhilarating moment, ready to take on whatever comes next.

Grayson Highlands 50K, May 4, 2024

Acknowledgements

This book wouldn't exist without the hours, days, weeks, months and years of logging miles with various runners who've crossed my path. To everyone I've run and trained with thank you for keeping me motivated and inspired. I've loved every minute of our conversations, every laugh, every run in the heat, cold, humidity, rain, snow, ice and even hurricane force winds. Special shoutout to my best running friends and our now extended group, the Cool Kids. All of you make me a better person.

Thanks to those runners I have never run with but motivated me to get better and believe in myself. You never know who you're inspiring on your solo runs, ultra races, sprint triathlons or track workouts. As Des Linden says, "Keep showing up".

To my coaches, Rhonda and Jenn, thank you for your belief and insight to make me a better runner. Your encouragement and faith kept me going when I was unsure if I could do your workouts or hit the paces you set out for me.

To Dr. Johnson and Dr. Graybar, plus Eric and Bruce, my Friday dream team, thank you for keeping me aligned, lasered and sane. Your tolerance for my wild running stories means the world.

Special thanks to our local Fleet Feet stores and especially to owner Michelle Moschet who has not only been my friend but also my advisor for all things shoes, running and nutrition. For dropping everything and helping me get new shoes when my feet were a mess of blisters and black toenails. Also, to Wendy and the staff for helping me with the shoe donations. Fleet Feet is much more than a running store, you're friends, mentors and family.

Joining the Wilmington Road Runners Club changed my life. I tell everyone to join a run club because your best friends are already there. Over the last 12 years, this amazing group has pushed me, supported me, and shaped me. And to Frank, our "mayor of running," thank you for the laughter and wisdom. You're a gem.

To my mom and dad: thank you for everything from cheering me on and donating to my causes, to taking care of the dogs and watching out for Scott. I thought having you across the street meant I'd take care of you, but it turns out you've been taking care of me all along.

Finally, Scott. My biggest fan. My calm in every storm. My anchor and co-pilot in this crazy life. You never complain when I wake you at 4:45 in the morning. You care for the dogs, hold down the fort, and remind me to rest. You've faced more pain than anyone should, and you've done it with grace and grit. Life hasn't unfolded exactly as we imagined, but I'm so proud of how we've walked it together. We make one hell of a team.

And to you, the reader. Thank you for picking up this book, for stepping into the miles with me, and for taking this journey through joy, heartbreak, grit, and triumph. Whether you're a runner or simply someone chasing a goal, I hope you found a bit of yourself in these pages. Keep going. You're stronger than you think.

ABOUT THE AUTHOR

ROBYN GODFREY is a World Major Marathon Six Star Finisher, a certified Level 1 Road Runners Club of America (RRCA) Running Coach, and a motivational speaker. She shares her passion for running and resilience through coaching, speaking engagements, and now, her writing. Robyn lives in Wilmington, North Carolina, with her husband, Scott, and their two spirited dogs, Bodie and Johnny. You can find her on Instagram @beachy_runner, or at www.robyngodfrey.com.

Robyn would love it if you'd take a photo and tag her on Instagram. She'd appreciate a review on Amazon and/or Good Reads too! Thank you for reading!

Printed in Dunstable, United Kingdom

68755232R00190